A Handful of Clay in the Potter's Hand

By Ipe Mathai

A Handful of Clay in the Potter's Hand

Life Changing Experiences of a Rebellious Runaway

Ipe Mathai

XP

A Handful of Clay in the Potter's Hand
by Ipe Mathai
Revised and updated edition 2008

Printed in the United States of America

ISBN 978-1-60647-619-2

This is a publication of:
Mathai Outreach Ministries Int.
P.O. Box 96495
Houston, Texas 77213-6495
U.S.A
Email: info@mathaioutreach.org
Website: www.mathaioutreach.org
Printed in the United States of America
Xulon Press
www.xulonpress.com

Dedication

This book is dedicated to all the
God-appointed people on my journey
who have helped impact and shape my life, faith,
profession, success
and ministry.

Acknowledgements

Susie, my life partner,
for your love, care, support and sacrifice through all
these years.
Our Children
Liz and Sarah,
for your continued love, support, respect and trust.
I am proud to see how God shaped you into beau-
tiful and strong women of faith.
Jacob,
Your unwavering faith in God makes me a proud
father.
Your support and your positive critique keeps me in
check and balance.
I am proud of you son.
Roy and Linda, for being God appointed spouses to
Liz and Jacob.
Our Grandchildren
Chris and Joel, for your love and smartness.
Sophia, my little princess for your gentleness and
affection and love.
I am proud to be your "Appachan."
And my brothers an sisters, for your
encouragement and support

Priscilla, for all the assistance and patience in this process.
Tiffany, for the critiquing of this book.
Above all,
The Almighty God for His steadfast love.

Foreword

I had the privilege to meet Ipe Mathai at a crucial junction of his life history, a young man, his eyes wide open, eager to learn, he entered the paramedical training course. A large vertical scar on his forehead made him look like a rebel. The scar was removed later by surgery, but Ipe Mathai remained a rebel against material, spiritual poverty and a fighter for human dignity.

Some thirty years later we met again, he was at the peak of his impressive social and economic success. He did not keep any of his achievements for himself. The results of his hard and determined work went to his family and to hundreds of deserving and ill people. And now, at the beginning of the third Millennium after the birth of Christ we met again. Aware of his own life experience he knows that material goods are not sufficient to help the poor and deserving people. To his socio-economic aid he adds spiritual and religious support.

The life history of Ipe Mathai is an impressive story of human determination and faith in God. His life will continue to provide material, spiritual, and religious resources to people in need. I wish him good success with God's help.

Dr. C. Heinz M.D
Baden, Switzerland

Foreword

Ipe Mathai and his family have attended Lakewood Church since the 70's and have been an integral part of our work here. His children grew up in the church, and Ipe is a Prayer Partner. This is a precious family, and I am glad to know them.

This book is wonderful, and it shows the love, mercy and compassion that the Lord has for His children. He is always there for us, to save, heal and deliver us, whatever the case may be. Ipe could have died from Hepatitis and could be blind today, but God!

Ipe Mathai is a very successful businessman, and he goes several times a year to India, to preach the Good News about Jesus to the villages where he grew up. We were thrilled to have part in buying a van there. Ipe's desire is to someday be full time in the ministry.

I trust that this book will bless you and help you to feel the heart of Ipe Mathai. He is a good man, and I salute him.

Dodie Osteen
Co-Founder Lakewood Church
Houston, Texas, USA

Introduction

A <u>HANDFUL OF CLAY IN THE POTTER'S HAND</u> is the story of the making of a man of God—through troubles, trials and tears—and through many triumphs. It is the story of God Almighty's work of redemption and restoration in the life of an individual. It is also the story of a unique call received in the life of an unlikely character whom God has chosen to express His manifold grace and miracle-working power in this generation.

That unlikely character is Mr. Ipe Mathai of the Lahayil Mathai Family in India. I too am a Mathai and Ipe is my younger brother. The name Mathai (Matthew) means the gift of God.

Being Ipe's elder brother, I too am an experiencer and empathizer of many of the events mentioned in the book, but the elements that made this story unique are his own—his calling, daring nature, and adventurous spirit coupled with a genuine compassion for the poor, sick & the lost.

I am glad to write this note because what Ipe Mathai has written in the narration of this book is part and parcel of our family's story which is fast becoming a legacy that we relish and cherish. The narration itself is unique in its simplicity, sincerity and sensitivity.

My humble prayer at this point is that this book and the story it portrays find its great and glorious end the Lord has intended! May this book continue to bless and influence many more thousands and bring unlimited glory to the Master Potter Himself!

Bishop Varghese L. Mathai, Th.D; Ph.D; LL.D.

Introduction

A *Handful of Clay in the Potter's Hand* tells the testimony of not just a man, but reveals the greatness of a masterful God. The stories and experiences of this book represent the clay that as you will read, began taking form. For there to be an actual vessel, the clay must go through an extensive process of forming and molding, and to pass the test, be put through the fire.

Some of the stories in this book are of joy, pain, victory, and trials. Just when you think there is no hope, you will notice that God, in all of His perfection, reshapes the clay in a new way. The most hopeless situation turns out to be a greater victory than the one before. The encouragement and inspiration from this book comes from the knowledge that God is still an amazing Potter that acts out of love and purpose for His greatest work of art yet-His children. His love is not limited to a certain select—His love transcends race, status, creed and culture. His love was able to reach a homeless person who did not live a godly life, and according to society, would never be a success. My Dad did not know he was on the Potter's wheel being prepared for a future of blessing and success—but God knew and with careful detail orchestrated his life to reveal His glory through it. I consider my Dad's life a true success story, but not just because of his merits and accomplishments. He was bold enough to yield his life to the will of God, and through his faithfulness and trust in God, he was and is blessed. If my father would have never surrendered to God, my life in turn, would have never been blessed.

To the reader, I ask that you allow this book to minister into your life. I have read this testimony many times by now and I have lived a part of it. It is amazing how God has encouraged my life personally through the reminders of His greatness in my Dad's testimony. The final chapter of this book has not yet come, God is still moving in a powerful way through my Dad's life. I am a witness to that and am able to experience new dimensions of God's love, firsthand. I have learned that God's best is usually beyond my comprehension and it is available to everyone that desires His perfect will. May this book open your eyes to the abounding love and grace of Jesus Christ.

In the Potter's Hands,
Sarah Ann Mathai, LMSW

"For I know the plans I have for you, declares the Lord, plans to prosper you and not to harm you, plans to give you a hope and a future." Jeremiah 29:11(NIV)

Preface

Handful of Clay in the Potter's Hand is about some of my life changing experiences and events that transformed a common person doing common things into one doing uncommon things for a noble cause. *"Does not the potter have the right to make out of the same lump of clay some pottery for noble purpose and some for common use." Romans 9:21 (NIV)*

Even though I came from a family of scholars and writers, my situation was different and unique. I had no desire or talent to write until one day the Holy Spirit started to pour out the memories of thoughts of the past with an aching heart and streams of tears from my eyes. So I claim this book was written with my tears. My path in life had events and experiences that changed the course of my life; a life filled with low esteem, rebellion, defeat, destruction, hopelessness, sickness, loss of sight and homelessness.

It was changed to a life with purpose, success, and fulfillment of God's promises to the generation to come. This is a story of a rebellious runaway who lived on the streets as a homeless person, but when God started to mold that person, he changed that hopeless person to a very successful professional, business executive, a humanitarian and a missionary evangelist.

As you unfold the story, you will see once I was poor and lived on the streets as a runaway, I was sick, broken-hearted and was rejected, I was in bondage to bad habits and spiritual darkness, and I lost sight in my right eye.

But when I accepted the free gift of Salvation through Jesus Christ, He set me free from all of these things, I now had a purpose and wanted to stand against the adversary and proclaim liberty in Jesus Christ to others. He gave me new dreams, hopes and promises to have a blessed future. God has planted within me a passion to serve Him.

He enabled me to start Mathai Outreach Ministries International to reach out to people in the same condition. My wife, Susie and I travel to many different countries with the Gospel of Jesus Christ, sharing the healing and delivering power of the Holy Spirit.

Besides doing mission work in India and neighboring countries in the 1040 window, I am able to serve our local community as a prayer partner and an ordained minister at Lakewood Church in Houston Texas.

Through our health care services, EHC Hospice, we are able to care and comfort the sick and dying and their families in the greater Houston area.

As a person who has gone through so much adversities in life, I can securely say that Jesus is the answer! I am encouraging anyone who is going through the hopeless and helpless condition that I was once in, to turn your life to a living and loving God, He is calling you to accept Him and He is willing to accept you just as you are. No matter what condition you are in, He can change your life!!!

This in not merely a success story or the American dream come true. It is a story of the fulfillment of God's promises in His children.

Blessings,
Ipe Mathai

Chapter 1

Here I begin

One Sunday afternoon in the summer of 1993, I was resting on my bed after attending a church service. Then, in a quiet voice, the Lord spoke to my heart. He said,
"Go Back to Your People."

I was at the peak of my life in every aspect in 1993. By this time, I had three profitable businesses with several million dollars in annual revenue. There were about 75 full-time and part-time employees in four offices in different parts of Texas as a part of my business. My responsibilities were even greater and we had a 200 to 300% growth annually.

I was actively involved in my church and local ministries and it seemed everything was finally falling into place. I had been supporting many ministries at that time, both here and abroad, especially in India.

But the voice said to go back to my people. Since all of my family members were in the United States, there didn't seem to be a reason for me to return to India. However, in obedience to this voice and His higher calling, I decided to go to India. Since that time I've returned once or twice every year to minister to the people of India.

The story of how I came to return to India as a Evangelist, rather than a citizen, is a miracle in and of itself. I faced disapproval of my family, homelessness, poverty, and illness in my quest to pursue God's call on my life. Not even I had fully understood what that call was until that afternoon. I was lying in my bed and the story came back to me of how God can use any piece of clay if it's willing to be worked by the Potters hand.

During a particular visit to India on April 21, 1998, I was flying on Air France from Paris to New Delhi. Having boarded the plane, I was browsing through the newspapers available there. An article in USA Today impressed me. It had a picture of a middle-aged man standing with both of his hands in his pockets; he was smiling. For some reason he held my attention. To me he seemed to express a feeling of satisfaction or contentment, maybe the sense of accomplishment. I'd met this man a few years back at a meeting of 350 entrepreneurs in Orlando, Florida. We shook hands and spent a few minutes talking at that meeting. He was Hugh McColl, the chairman of the merged Bank America and Nations Bank, one of the US's largest coast-to-coast banks. He was a very simple man and I considered my meeting him a rare and pleasant privilege.

Mr. McColl's calm, composed and satisfied look caused me to begin thinking about what I had accomplished in my life. As I began to think back, my mind was flooded with memories of my past. Mr. McColl was an ordinary person achieving extraordinary things.

With all that I had experienced I could see the mighty hand of God behind all of my personal accomplishments and experiences, both physical and spiritual. As I thought, I took a piece of paper and began to write down the list of trials and accomplishments in my own life.

I reflected on the person who would lead a life filled with low self-esteem, and unacceptable behavior, and very poor accomplishments. A person who wondered if he has any hope or future, but then that person finding the path of life which led to success, family, friends, financial abundance, acceptance and achievement. Then to come to a place where my life had a purpose, my life was full of promises. And I knew I was in a place where I was able to help others with my life.

I was overwhelmed by these thoughts as they poured into my mind and out my pencil. Through tears I began to thank God for his loving kindness and his promises.

While my present was full of rejoicing, some of the memories of the past reminded me just how far I had come with God's help.

The Early Years

I was the second of six children in my family. My parents were reputable, scholarly, high achievers in our society. My father was a well-known schoolteacher, author, and poet. My mother was a housewife. We lived on a large farm, at least large for our area. The family farms in India are not like those in America. Many farms in India are merely a few acres of land to cultivate and produce food items and crops like rice paddy, tapioca, sugarcane, pepper, coconut trees, banana plants, and vegetable gardens. At that time many people in our area did not have land like we had. There were many poor people who lived around us who were laborers.

As one of the older children, I would occasionally help my father on the farm. I also helped my mother in the kitchen very often when she was sick from the effects of asthma. Since this responsibility fell on me often had to prepare meals.

One evening while I was in the kitchen preparing food, there was a terrible accident. I was deep frying "pappadam". Pappadam is a very thin flatbread made with lentil flour often made crisp by deep frying. I was cooking it when suddenly

21

it caught fire and exploded to a large flame. I was frightened and began to panic. My father responded to my cries for help and ran into the kitchen. He removed the pot of boiling oil. It spilled over me and ran down me from the top of my head, down my half naked body. Blisters sprang up on my forehead, head, eyebrows, hands, chest, abdomen, and legs. My father saw what happened and grabbed a jug of water and dumped it over me. The pain was excruciating I could do nothing more than scream.

Everyone panicked. Suddenly chaos erupted in the kitchen as neighbors and family members flooded in and out. I was in severe pain but no one could do anything for me. In those days there was not even a hospital nearby let alone a telephone, ambulance, or emergency room where I could have found relief. When the chaos settled a friend went to a local physician, the only one in town, and he treated me with ointment and bandages. I had second and third degree burns covering my body and my only treatment was to lie still in bed for a number of days in a hot, sticky climate where air conditioning did not exist. Most of the wounds healed fast but there were deep scars on my skin, and deeper scars on my heart.

This led to an inferiority complex. As a result I became rebellious, very independent, and mischievous. My older brother, Joy, (Dr. Varghese L. Mathai) was a very gentle and smart person and was liked by all. His gentle nature, and academic success, was in stark contrast to the rebel I was becoming. I was an average student who seemed to lack manners and self-control. The more people compared the two of us, the less I measured up.

Then I learned to smoke beedi and later moved on to cigarettes. In a traditional, reputable, Christian family no one smoked or drank. Usually the children in these families were also very polite. My behavior and habits brought disgrace to my family and cost me their respect. Because of my behavior

I was moved from the forefront of my family life and put in the background. That led to me seeking approval from people other than my family.

Eventually I did find such a group. It was a gang known as *the Eight and a Half Company.* This group consisted of youth from my neighborhood who were as wild as I was. As we grew up so did our activities. In addition to smoking we stole toddy from palm trees and drank. I also began to steal to support my habits and to fit in to the group's activities.

Stealing was unacceptable not only to my family, but to society in general. I began with stealing small amounts of money from home. Sometimes I would lie to my parents in order to get a few coins from them. They grew increasingly frustrated with my behavior but no amount of punishment seemed to change me. They tried spanking me with a stick and other discipline. My mother once resorted to tying me up for stealing a quarter rupee. While the amount of money wasn't much, about enough to purchase a lunch for a child, the principle was what mattered. This was not the first time I'd stolen from them. It had become habitual and my parents wanted it stopped.

It was the post World War II period and there was scarcity everywhere in the newly independent India. We had just been liberated from British rule in 1945 and the country was extremely poor because they did not leave much wealth behind when they left. There were very little resources and very high demand. There was rationing of kerosene, sugar, rice, clothes, and other necessities. The worst, however, was the scarcity of jobs throughout the country.

During that time a great deal of Communist propaganda entered the country and many poor, unemployed people were attracted to Marxism, even though it was outlawed. The growth of Communism in Kerala led to it being the second state in India to elect a communist government. E.M.S. Nampoothiripad and M.N. Govindan Nair, the stalwarts, were the leaders of the underground communist activities in Kerala.

I had been interested in politics since my early teens. Besides being an enthusiastic National Congress worker, I was also associated closely with Arathimukku Congress party at Pandalam, my hometown. My involvement in politics kept me from my studies, which resulted in bad grades.

From 1958-1959, I actively participated in the Vimochana Samaram, anti-government activities to topple the Communist government. We boycotted our schools and assembled at the party office, near N.S.S. College Pandalam, to plan our future course of action. We would ambush the busses using roadblocks and would even stone them. Although the police chased us away, we continued our activities. That resulted in me being put in jail three times.

Since the government could not feed all the prisoners, we were quickly released. Sometimes the police released us far away from our homes so that we would have to walk long distances to reach home. This went on for almost eighteen months. This led to further tension at home.

Sometimes I stayed at home, other times I stayed other places. Many times, I had to sleep in the attic. There was no peace in our home. My father was very dominant and when things didn't go his way, he would become angry. This led to quarrels and fights. My mother, by contrast, was very calm and quiet, but there were many times when my father was verbally abusive and blamed my mother for my behavior. We often quarreled at home about my habits, character, political activities, and the way I lived. My mother was the unfortunate casualty of these quarrels.

My absence from home was reason enough for quarrels, but my presence made them worse. The lack of peace at home made everyone unhappy.

Once, when I was fifteen years old, a group of young boys from the village gathered by the roadside under a streetlight to discuss their achievements, failures, and plans for the future. In those days the young people could only look forward to joining the armed forces, becoming a teacher, a clerk, or a worker in the field after finishing high school or college. At that time, a clerical job with the government in the state of Kerala, earned 79 Rupees per month. That was approximately the same as the minimum wage in the US. There would be hundreds of applicants for just one position. However, even before someone could apply for it the position would have secretly been filled.

A few of my friends who had gathered under that streetlight had specific plans and were on track to accomplishing them. As for me, the youngest of the group, I could not say much about the future because I had not developed any special skills or talents. I was not very smart in school, although I somehow earned passing grades. My handwriting was bad and my vocabulary was poor, even in our own vernacular, Malayalam.

On the other hand, my older brother was outstanding and was appreciated for his English, good handwriting and behavior. Naturally, my parents expected me to be like him, but I could not meet their expectations.

My parents had high hopes for us. They wanted us to be professionals. Unfortunately, my environment wasn't healthy. I led a miserable life and most of our family friends disapproved of my behavior. Even I did not accept myself because I felt helpless to change. I wanted to end my life, but thankfully God had other plans.

Chapter 2

Attempts to Escape

W hen I was in junior high school, I ran away from home for the first time. Someone who knew my father found me, brought me back home, and put me back in school. I eventually did finish high school and I enrolled at the local college close to my home. Somehow I finished one year in college, but my aimless, unproductive, and unhappy life continued. Had I continued, I could have received a Bachelor's Degree but I had no ambition to do that.

I planned to run away again and came up with a better plan, not like the one from junior high. During the summer of 1961, I made my master plan. In order to have enough money for my travel and immediate expenses, I sold my college books and some of my family's gold jewelry. Altogether, I made 22.50 Rupees, which was not too much. I took an extra pair of clothes and a bed sheet to cover myself with while sleeping. Then, one evening, before my father came back from work, I left home. I made sure no one followed me. I didn't' take the regular routes. I walked and crossed the river and went to the bus stop that we normally did not use.

Thus, I could escape from my home unnoticed. From there, instead of taking a train, I took a boat and finally I reached a big city named Cochin. My aim was to join the Air Force.

Job Searching as a Runaway

At the recruiting center, I stood in a line with thousands of other young men who had come to enlist. The Air Force Officer who did the initial screening came to me and at the very first look said, "Son, you need to grow up a little more. Go home and eat well." I did not say a word to him, but left and decided my first day of job searching was over. That night I boarded a train to go to whatever the next city was. I did not know where I was going. When I got off the train the next morning, my bed sheet was missing. I had lost my most valuable possession.

That morning I met a man who seemed to know the city. While I was talking to him, he told me that a factory would be opening soon and he knew the people in charge there. He assured me that with his influence he would get me a job. He even had an application form with him. He filled it out for me so he could take it directly to the people in charge. In exchange, he wanted some money, which he knew I had.

I was reluctant, but I gave him some. Shortly after he got the money he said that he had to visit someone and that he would be back within thirty minutes. I waited for him a long time but when he did not return, I knew I would not be getting a factory job anytime soon. My second day of job searching was over.

Next I went to Northern Kerala to a town named Wynadu. I tried to find day labor work there but I was too small for physical labor. Furthermore, I didn't have the necessary skills for other jobs. I left Wynadu and spent the next month living at the railway stations and city bus stands in the area.

I often bought a newspaper in the morning, read it, and then when it got hot during the day I'd hold it over my head to block the sun. Then I'd use that same newspaper at night to sleep on. I passed the time by walking for miles along roads and on train tracks. Sometimes I managed to get on the train without tickets and go from place to place.

Finally, I ended up in Kasargod, the northern tip of Kerala. My pockets were nearly empty and I was desperate to find a job.

At last, I found a job as a table boy in a large restaurant. My job was cleaning tables and collecting plates. I earned enough money to be able to eat and buy my cigarettes. The restaurant where I worked provided all the food and there was an open water tap where I could get buckets of water to bathe in. I was even offered a place to sleep with the other workers, so it seemed that all my immediate needs were met.

I was offered a job as a waiter at another restaurant. I did a good job there, but the restaurant was sold. Since the management had other restaurants, they offered me a job at one in Mangalore, near the bus station. I went there thinking that it would be good to be in a new city, with a new language and perhaps unknown opportunities. Unfortunately there I had not place to sleep.

Late in the night, when most passengers had left, the bus station would be empty. Along with other employees, and sometimes even with cows or dogs, I slept on the floor there. It was a very crowded bus station so there were always people coming and going. Occasionally I was able to sleep on one of the various concrete benches. This went on for about eighteen months. I was quite comfortable and happy there because there was not one to complain and no one to listen to.

It was during this period that I made many friends-bus drivers, porters, and restaurant workers among them. Most of them liked me because I had passed high school and I could read and write English and Malayalam, something many of them could not do. They needed my help to write letters to their parents and families. When my parents sent me to school, I was not interested in studying, but now I decided I wanted to learn something. I started taking classes at a typing institute for one hour a day. It was there that I met a person from Kerala named Mukundan. He told me about an institution that was accepting applications for paramedical training. Although the last date to accept the application had passed, he encouraged me to take a chance. I did not know where the place as so I asked one of the bus drivers who came to the restaurant to take me there. He agreed to drop me off because it was on his route.

After I entered Father Muller's Hospital, I went down a long driveway until I finally reached a separate compound within the larger compound called St. Joseph's Leprosy Asylum. It was a separate facility within the larger institution. Most of the patients staying there were chronically sick and crippled and stayed for a very long time. I walked through the hallway to the end of the building there in a small office with just a table and a chair sat a tall, white young man who would impact the course of my life; He was Christoph Heinz, M.D.

Going to this interview and meeting with him was a big step in my life. For more than two years I had lived on the streets. Going to an institution and meeting with a white man was both exciting and intimidating. I was hopeful, but unsure of anything. I also knew very little spoken English which made me even more nervous, but as we spoke, I realized that he also spoke very little English.

It was a leprosy hospital that was well-maintained and clean, but the smell in the halls was like Nursing homes today.

I walked in to his room wearing a single piece dhoti and a short sleeved blue shirt that was too big for me. I had exchanged my good shirt with someone who needed it. I had no shoes or slippers on. He raised his head and looked at me. He did not say anything because he was not expecting me.

"I am an employee and I'm looking for a job." I said. Then he directed me to his Secretary, Greta, and returned to his work.

Greta was a very pretty, gracious young lady, but her feet were deformed and was crippled and she required supportive devices to walk. She took the time to give me an application and helped me fill it out properly. Then I turned it in.

I thought there was no hope of being admitted because the deadline had passed three days earlier. Nevertheless, I received a card in the mail informing me I'd been accepted to the paramedical program. I had to support myself for the first two months, then the Hospital would pay me a stipend of 60 Rupees per month. That would be enough for my barest needs, including my cigarettes, but did not leave any extra money for other necessities. I shared my problem with a couple of restaurant employees who wished to see me doing something better and they collected a few rupees for me.

When the management of the restaurant discovered that I was going to leave for the training they fired me. With almost a month before I was supposed to leave for the program, I had nowhere to go, no money, and no place to live. I found a group of laborers (collies) who worked with stones. I got acquainted with them and they gave me a chance to work with them and live in their tents. I accepted their offer and worked with them for a few days. Without complaining, I carried stones on my head. Even if I had complained there was not one to listen to me.

Chapter 3

Newly found profession

Finally, the time came and I moved to Fr. Muller's Hospital in Kankanady, Mangalore to start my paramedical training. I still had the same single dhothi and the oversized blue shirt I wore my first time there. I had to wash them every evening so I could wear it the next day.

One day I met a Poojari (priest) in a Hindu temple who was one of the candidates accepted for the paramedical training Program. His name was Thankappan. He was an intelligent person and had worked as a Poojari in a temple in Karnataka for many years. We decided to go together and rent the front room of a shop near Father Muller's Hospital.

I cannot go on without saying a little bit about the organization that accepted me as their trainee. It was the Federation Emmaus Swiss Leprosy Relief Organization, made up of voluntary medical professionals. It was a non-religious organization from Switzerland working in collaboration with Fr. Muller's Hospital and St. Joseph's Leprosy Hospital. It was one of their first projects in India. The project leader was Dr. Christoph Heinz, M.D. He had come to Vellore and Karigiri,

India, learned about the disease of leprosy, and was part of the Eradication Program.

The paramedical classes started on August 1, 1963. In the beginning, most of the day was spent in the classroom studying Anatomy, Physiology, and Microbiology. We gradually started to work with other staff members and instructors of various departments. Even though I did not understand much, Dr. Heinz often referred to Dr. Chochrane's book, the textbook for medical schools about leprosy. Dr. Heinz trained in Karigiri along with Dr. V.P. Macaden. From the time the Paramedical Training Program started we had a group of very good instructors from different disciplines. Among them was Mr. Conrad Edge, a fine young man from Dunon, Scotland. Dr. Modayil, Dr. Choeilo, Dr. Pinto and Sister Edmond from the Sisters of Charity School of Nursing. Some of the students as well as instructors came from Sisters of Charity and Fr. Muller's Hospital, Kankanady. As the course of study started and progressed I got quite busy and interested in what I was studying.

The agreement was that I had to pass a test after the first thirty days in order to begin to receive the stipend. I was fully depending on the stipend to be able to survive. Therefore, I needed to study very hard. My roommate, Thankappan, the ex-Poojari insisted on going to sleep early and turned the light off at night. Then he would wake up in the middle of the nigh and study while I was sound asleep. Somehow I passed the initial exams and qualified for the stipend, but I still had to live another month before I would receive the first payment. It was a real struggle but somehow I managed.

One morning while Thankappan and I were going to the hospital, we heard a soft voice behind us. A young boy, maybe five years old, was calling us in Tulu, the language of South Canara. I looked back and recognized him. He was our neighbor's son, sent by his mother for a rupee. I had only one rupee, which was for my meal that day. I had not eaten breakfast yet. I gave that one rupee to the boy. He ran home happily with the money, which was to be used for breakfast for four children, the father, and the mother. At that moment I felt good, but a fear followed. "How can I be in class all day without eating anything?" Yet we went to the Brahmin's coffee shop, had our breakfast and told him that we would pay later.

My First Miracle

Something unusual happened that day. The postman was looking for me for the first time in two years. He had a money order for me for fifty rupees. It was a total surprise! I had not written to my parents nor to any of my relatives, but after investigating, I found out that my roommate had somehow gotten my home address and had written a letter informing my family where I was. This was my first miracle and it was quite unexpected. I had just given the Karnataka boy my last rupee and that same day I received fifty rupees before lunchtime. I had never even heard of such miracles before!

My Religious Experience

As far as having a religious background, I really did not remember a whole lot about church other than attending the Marthoma Church's Sunday school. I never wanted to go with my parents even though my parents were both God-fearing people.

We had a Marthoma Church on the west side, an Orthodox Church on the north side, a Catholic Church on the south side and an Orthodox cross and offering center on the east side. In fact, when it was said loudly we could hear the kurbana (Mass) from our home! My family belonged to the Marthoma Church. I remember attending Sunday school when I was young. I might have learned a lot of Bible stories there but I did not remember any of them.

As I grew up, I did not quit going to Church. Even though I was a rebellious kid, I not only went to the Marthoma Church but also to the Orthodox Church and the Catholic Church. Many of my friends were Hindus and Muslims so I often went to Hindu temples, especially for the Aattam festival. The Aattam festival is a cultural religious act with a costumed dancer.

Even though Hindu temples prohibited entrance to Christians and Muslims, my friends always protected me. I had never changed my faith because I really did not have a solid one.

In 1956, when my older brother, Joy, got saved, he used to lead the family prayer meeting. Because of my rebellious attitude and smoking habits I could not pray with anybody. I was exposed to church when I was about 4 or 5 years old when I stayed with one of my aunts and her family. Her husband was our "Appachan". An Appahan is an elderly man or grandfather. He was also an evangelist in the Marthoma Church. That was a traditional protestant church. Every morning and every evening they had family prayer time. It was compulsory for us to participate in it. So I could say I'd been raised in a Christian home.

After I ran away from home, I sometimes attended an Episcopalian Church at Mangalore. Most of the people who attended it wore suit coats on Sundays. I could not go there for a long time because I never had a coat to wear. Sometimes, I would attend the Basal Mission Church. While I was in Mangalore I wanted to go to a Catholic church. I always worked with nuns who belonged to Sisters of Charity. The Mother Superior was a nun from Kerala. She liked me because I too was Malayalee. Many times I was invited to the convent lobby for coffee and snacks. Many of the nuns were my instructors or fellow students. They were nice and pious people who always invited me to mass. They always included me in their functions and sincerely cared about me.

Rev. Fr. Fernandez, the Director of the entire Fr. Muller's Hospital system was a Catholic Priest, and a nice and able administrator. One day Rev. Fr. Fernandez died and his funeral was one of the greatest Catholic funerals I had ever seen. A citywide procession was held with his casket. Then his body was buried inside the Hospital Chapel.

A few days after the burial of Rev. Fr. Fernandez, a senior nun, Sr. Leonard was comforting the bereaved employees. She said, "Fr. Fernandez was a Holy man and now he's a saint in heaven. If we need any favor form God we can pray to Father Fernandez and he will pray to the Holy Mother Mary who will in turn pray to Jesus Christ and he will pray to the Heavenly Father."

She was very sincere in telling that but when I heard it I started to think it was a pretty complex way to receive a favor from God, or even to get an answer to my prayers. Of course, I was brought up as a protestant where it was taught that we could pray directly to God through Jesus Christ instead of going through saints.

1Timothy 2:5 "For there is one God and one mediator between God and men, the man Jesus Christ."

When we worked for Fr. Fernandez, we knew him to be an able administrator and priest, but I had a hard time connecting a human being to God's place.

While he was living I couldn't remember receiving favors from him, now that he was dead how could I expect more? I wondered how much priority he'd give my prayers. This idea took root in me and was one of the things that kept me from becoming a catholic. It was also, possibly, the first time I considered the deeper issues of faith.

During the training program we had combined sessions with the student nurses from Father Muller's hospital. There were about 120 young women along with the paramedical students. Conrad Edge, a registered physiotherapist from Scotland, was teaching anatomy and physiology. He asked me questions about some muscle functions and I answered with what I felt was the correct answer based on what he'd taught us in class. Although my answer was correct, he told me that I was wrong and asked me to sit down. Everyone watched me as I sat down. Suddenly I was keenly aware of the outfit that I'd worn every day to school as well as the ugly scar across my forehead. I was a young man and to fail so miserably in front of peers, many of them young ladies, was quite a blow. I sat down quietly and wished I was invisible.

The next day when Conrad came to the class he asked me to stand up in front of everyone. The sting of the previous day's humiliation was still fresh and I wondered what purpose it would serve to have me stand a second time.

"Class," he began, "Ipe is the only one who understands what I'm teaching all of you. Yesterday he was the only one to correctly answer my question."

I was astonished.

"You may sit down, Ipe."

I returned to my seat, much more confident in my abilities. That evening a group of students came to me asking for help. When they had doubts or didn't understand what we were studying in anatomy and physiology they came to me. For the first time in my life someone approved of me and appreciated me for something.

Not only did fellow students have confidence in me but the instructors also saw my potential and entrusted me with various tasks. I started to learn new techniques in a hospital environment including doing some work with leprosy patients. I was enthusiastic about my work. There were many tasks to caring for Leprosy patients and I enjoyed them all. Sometimes all the person needed was someone to talk to. Other patients needed medicine or to have their wounds cleaned. Whatever way I served, I never complained. It was then that I was introduced to the concept of working hard for humanitarian concerns. I began to feel that caring for people would become part of my life. I never refused to help a person, no matter my job description.

When I completed my paramedical training in April 1964 Dr. Heinz called the group of students who had passed into his office to congratulate us.

"I have selected Ipe and Mukundan to work with me." Dr. Heinz said. Out of the 13 students who completed the training, only two of us had been asked to work for Swiss Emmaus in Mangalore the rest had to go out and find other jobs. It was a shock to all of them. I was excited, and surprised, to be selected to be a part of the Emmaus team, but I didn't know what to say to those who had not been chosen.

By that time Dr. Heinz's family had been in India almost 2 years and they were getting ready to go on furlough but before he left he arranged for the two of us to go to Chevayur Leprosy Hospital. There we would spend six months doing further training under Dr. Harris from England who was doing research on leprosy in Calicut.

In Calicut I worked with Dr. Harris and his team of health professionals from different parts of the world. We were given a house to live in and were paid a good salary by the Swiss Emmaus Association. He entrusted me with many special research projects. There, under his guidance, I found a new technique to treat calluses. I became known as the "callous king."

For the first time since I had left home, I went to see my loved ones. I could not explain to my father what I was doing because I had not become a doctor as he planned. Paramedical, despite the similar name, are not paramedics. We were trained to do clinical and research work. We also worked as health workers in the villages. Despite not knowing what I did, my father did not dare to ask me anything because he knew that I was bold enough to do what I wanted to do. Although he was not proud, and he was happy that I had found something in life and I was very happy with my profession. After spending a few weeks of a joyful vacation with them, I went back to Mangalore.

By this time Dr. Heinz had returned and we started concentrating on the village work. He appointed me to being in charge of the village work. In the following months we started up five out station clinics. Every day I had a certain time to work in the clinic. In addition, I taught the villagers prevention methods in their language, Kannada and Tulu. Our programs were well accepted in the rural areas. Because of that I became one of the valuable team member in the organization.

Many new people from Switzerland as well as other European countries started coming to work with various projects in Mangalore. My project was doing quite well. New technicians and researchers came and targeted certain specialties. I was a good source of information for them. They came to India, stay for six to twenty-four months to train others, and then went back to their countries.

In 1965, a young physician named Dr. Macaden came with his wife Susan, who was also a doctor. Dr. Heinz had received training under Dr. Macaden in Karigiri near Vellore. Both were very committed practitioners and aggressive, especially in the research for the eradication of leprosy.

I worked with Dr. Heinz as one of the most trustworthy members of the team. As the work progressed, many more people were added to the organization. My clinical responsibilities increased and I was still concentrating mostly on the village fieldwork. Dr. Macaden had become my direct supervisor and medical officer. He had already managed hundreds of paramedical in Tamilnadu and had come to Mangalore, which was comparatively a smaller project.

One evening, as my friends and I were walking in Kankanady we saw a leprosy patients sitting on the sidewalk. The next morning when I went the same way I saw them in the same place and he looked worse than he had the previous day. I brought him to the hospital. Since Dr. Heinz knew what I was doing, I did not consult Dr. Macaden. It caused a little friction because Dr. Macaden did not want to admit the patient and wondered if I'd taken a bribe in order to do so. I was a bit hurt by his decision not to admit the patient. I took the matter to Dr. Heinz and he saw the problem by recommending me to Dr. Macaden. After that we work together for years with mutual respect and held each other in high regard. Even though he was my direct boss, he and Susan cared for me as a younger brother.

When Dr. Heinz returned to Switzerland, Dr. Wintch and his wife Leena came to replace them. Both of these doctors were specialists; he a plastic surgeon and she a dermatologist. I worked with the both of them. Dr. Wintch was a quiet person. He could be in an operating room for several hours at a time without saying a single word. I became his first assistant in surgery. Dr. Leena Wintch introduced several new pharmacological preparations and taught me how to prepare them. Since I was with these three specialists, I was exposed to three specialized areas of medicine at the same time.

When I was not in surgery at the hospital I traveled to the villages with Dr. Macaden exploring new fields. We exchanged our ideas, in medicine and the humanities. Two to three years went by like that. And one day he suggested that I get further training so I could do more things. I'm sure that the suggestion had come from the Swiss Emmaus and other senior members of the organization. I met with Dr. Ferrin, the president of the Swiss Emmaus Association, and the General Secretary Mr. Rosenfield. They were both happy with my performance.

At this time the Swiss Emmaus work at Mangalore was recognized by the government of Karnataka. The governor of Karnataka, Mr. V.V. Giri, who later became the President of India, visited the hospital at Kankanady. When he was there I had the opportunity to meet him and shake his hand.

It was a real pleasure to work with such a wonderful group of people. Each of them had committed their lives to alleviating the pain and suffering of many people. They worked tirelessly and it was that work ethic, and desire to serve, that would help me achieve greater things in life later on.

Going to Nursing school, My experience in Nagercoil

The Swiss Emmaus offered to send me to any medical professional school I wanted, and I chose to study nursing. They sent me with full pay and never ask me to sign a bond, contract, or agreement. We checked out several places that offered male nursing. I selected the Salvation Army Catherine Booth Hospital School of Nursing in Nagercoil Tamil Nadu. Before I left for nursing school in June of 1968, Dr. Macaden warned me that I was on my own and they could not influence another institution.

Although I had excellent recommendations from an international organization, my SSLC certificate, (a cumulative report of the entire time in high school) revealed who I had been in my younger days, which was not at all good. Admission to this nursing program was based only upon merit and my SSLC book did not show much merit. However, I still got a conditional admission stating that if I did not do well for the first three months I would be kicked out.

For me this meant a new organization and its philosophy, a new religious association, and a new local language,

Tamil. There were also very strict rules twenty-four hours a day. In addition to all these other differences, there were also differences in social structure. At the Catherine Booth Hospital most of the managerial staff were Anglo foreigners, which meant there were cultural differences. There are also differences between Salvation Army students and non-salvation army students. I was not used any of these things. In Mangalore we had a great deal of freedom. White foreigners and locals worked together and had fun together. Here the morning started with hostel food, seniority struggles in the hostel, and compulsory chapel service. Then, as we went to the wards or classrooms, there was vast parity between seniors and juniors.

Even though I had enjoyed freedom in the past, there was not much of that freedom in Nagercoil. This was the first time in my life that I had to live in a dormitory and that in itself had its own rules and regulations. The staff and the senior students demanded respect and a certain amount of obedience from juniors. Since I had worked, earned my salary, and spent it the way I liked for years, this was a bit hard for me to adjust to. Most of them understood that and I was not really pushed around much by the seniors.

Our day started with standing in lines to be able to use the bathrooms. The food we had to eat was not good. Compulsory chapel service followed, and then work. The thing I liked least was that we had to wear a dhoti instead of pants, something I was not used to, especially in my first year. A dhoti is a long piece of untailored white cloth which is wrapped around the waist and goes all the way down to the feet. It is similar to a woman's skirt.

When I came to Nagercoil I already had the habit of smoking. If they were to find out about my smoking habit, I was sure they would expel me the very first week. Yet I could not stop, so I secretly smoked for a few more days. The life of the junior student was monitored so much and there was no room for many of the habits I had. I knew that I would need to break my bad habits if there was any chance of me lasting in school.

The biggest achievement

Maybe for the first time in my life, I really needed help beyond what man could do for me. I was tired of the freedom I had enjoyed. I was, in fact, looking for some kind of control. I cried out to God for the first time in my life. I told him I didn't want the freedom I'd once had and I did not want to continue smoking.

I realized I had an opportunity to change my life. If I continued smoking I was going to lose everything. In those days there were no treatment centers like we now have and I knew that I could not stop by myself. On the afternoon of June 22, 1968, while I still had a good supply of cigarettes, I made a decision: I would never smoke again. I cried out to God to help me and threw all the cigarettes away. I never smoked again. I realized then that God had heard my cry.

For the first time I realized that God listens to the cries of desperate people and comes in and helps. I had stopped smoking before but substituted it with sniffing and chewing. Then, after a short period, I ended up having all of those bad habits together. However, this time God miraculously took away all of my cravings for tobacco. I learned that I was the one who had to take the first step to do anything. Everyone else would advise, pray, disgrace, physically threaten, or even hate you, but when God does things he does it in a way that is so kind, loving, and perfect. Later on I read about it in *Psalms 40:1,2 (KJV) "He heard my cry and brought me up out of a horrible pit."*

First, I felt the freedom from the bondage of smoking, which I'd never felt before. I did not have to lower myself to do things in order to smoke. I didn't have to hide from others, steal from home, or borrow money from people. It was not a small thing for me to be able to stop smoking. Smoking had made me a prodigal son and led me to do other things my family and culture did not approve of.

The life I had lived was without much discipline but here it was different. In nursing school life was lived with strict rules in a controlled environment. It was highly disciplined with strict religious rules and we were always under the watchful eyes of others. New students had to watch how they walked, talked...every action. There was no room for inappropriate words or deeds.

After a busy schedule at the school we were expected to return to our dormitories where the seniors demanded respect from the younger students. Despite the strict rules, or maybe because of them, I now felt there was meaning to life, something I had never felt before. The first three months passed and I took several tests. I passed all of them, which meant my probation period was over. Finally I was accepted into the regular program.

The first year of studies went by without many problems. I always remembered the words of Dr. Macaden, "You are on your own. We don't have any responsibility for your education." Of course, they were sending my salary check from my paramedic job and because of that I didn't have to struggle financially. In fact, I was the only student who had plenty of money to spend after paying tuition and other expenses. I passed the final exams the first year and was first in my class.

Nursing education was not bad, but it was hard. I worked eight hours a day in the wards with patients. There I learned many procedures and techniques. When I was not working, I attended classes.

In addition to my studies, something else was going on in my life. I had a desire to know God and a thirst to belong to him. After the first six months of school we were given a month-long vacation. That was December 1968. For my vacation I chose to go home to Pandalam.

When I arrived home everyone asked what I was doing. Even though this was not even close to what my father had wanted, he never opposed me because he knew that I was not depending on him. Moreover, I had done a number of brave things and I was not going to listen to anyone about what I was doing.

Chapter 4

Newly found faith

During this trip my family started to notice changes in my life. I no longer smoke and I showed I had a clear direction in my life. While things were happening in my life, the Lord was doing a lot of things in my family as well. He was touching each of them individually. My elder brother, Joy, was already a born-again Christian. Then my sister Leelamma got saved, received Jesus, and began living a strong Christian life. Then my sister Susamma and my mother got saved. Unfortunately, this did not bring joy to my father. He'd had big plans for his children and since our lives had taken another route he'd become a very disappointed man.

The church in our home was like the early church as described in *Acts 2:42. "They devoted themselves to the apostles teaching and to the fellowship, to the breaking of bread and to prayer."*

As a newly born-again Christian family, our priorities changed from physical needs to spiritual needs. We separated more time learning the word of God, praying, and fellowshipping with other Christians even though there was no formal church in our area. New believers assembled in our home to worship and we invited senior pastors and prophets from different places to come teach and edify the body of Christ. We fed the people who came and provided money for their transportation. This became a practice for us.

My sister, Leelamma, was a full-time graduate student when God got a hold of her. Suddenly she was extreme in her faith and school became less important to her. She was anointed by the Holy Spirit with the gifts of healing and casting out demons and because of her determination, faith, and strong anointing, a lot of changes took place in our home. Later she finished her master's degree and a degree in theology.

Susamma, my youngest sister, was always concerned about hospitality and she worked very hard with my mother. My sisters were like Mary and Martha. Many people came to our home to preach, fast, pray, eat, and rest. Coming back from nursing school, I found all of this very new and different. I wondered how they could spend so much time feeding other people when our family had always lived in scarcity. Leelamma explained to me that the lands we had worked for years were producing more than they ever had.

When we were all at home, we work hard to cultivate Paddy (rice). The harvest we brought in every year was only enough to last us eight or nine months. Even though we'd cultivated a large area of land we'd have to buy rice four months out of the year. Either by drought or floods most of the crops were damaged or lost.

Now that the family was honoring the Word, spending time in prayer, and providing food for the hungry, my family had rice to spare despite cultivating a smaller area of our farm. With this small area they had so much that they were able to sell rice and get money for the first time. I thought about that. Later on I realized how true the word of God was *Luke 6:38 "Give, and it will be given to you. A good measure, pressed down, shaken together and running over, will be poured into your lap. For with the measure you use it, it will be measured to you."* I also learned many people had been praying for my salvation. My brother Joy wrote a note to my mother saying that I would be saved before the end of that year. One day during my vacation there was a cottage meeting in my house and the pastor preached about salvation. I still didn't understand what he was talking about, despite having been born in a Christian family. That night when the pastor gave an altar call, I raised my hand to accept Jesus as my personal savior and Lord with the prayer of repentance. Then they prayed for me. This was on December 22, 1968.

One day another brother in Christ from the church, led by the Spirit, told me about a meeting at Thiruvalla. It was at his brother's house. I said that I would go with him. Pastor A.T. Thomas preached a sermon on baptism but, as usual, I did not understand much. Finally he asked me if I wanted to get baptized. I told him if it was the Word of God and it was a commandment to be baptized after accepting salvation I wanted to. I had not gone prepared for baptism so they brought me a change of clothes. We all gathered at a beloved sister's large house at Mepral where there was water.

"I was baptized in water in the Name of the Father, and of the Son, and of the Holy Spirit." This fulfilled the command of Jesus Christ as written in *Mark 16:16. "Whoever believe and is baptized will be saved, but whoever does not believe will be condemned."*

That was on December 31, 1968.

One week after I was baptized I had to go back to Nagercoil to continue my nursing program. I have never seen the pastor who led me to salvation or the pastor who baptized me since then. I went on my way rejoicing as written in ***Acts 8:36-39." Look, here is water.. Why shouldn't I be baptized? ....but went on his way rejoicing."***

When I returned to Nagercoil I was a changed person. I was born-again and baptized. It wasn't until I returned to nursing school that I realized how much had changed. Many of my new beliefs were not in line with practices at Catherine Booth Hospital.

Kerala Pentecostal churches imposed many restrictions on believers, some of them were more tradition than scriptural, but I was happy to adhere to them to keep my newly found faith.

Even though the Salvation Army is a Christian organization there were differences between what they taught and my Pentecostal experience. I wasn't able to pray in tongues or pray for supernatural intervention. This made it difficult for a new Pentecostal believer like me. Even though I was with many Salvation Army people, my best friend, Chacko, was a born-again believer. I met a few others with similar experiences in the compound and we got together to fellowship. Brother Chacko and I always tried to go to gospel meetings as well.

At one of those meetings I met Dr.Varghese a doctor from Vellore living in the staff quarters. He had had a similar born-again experience. We became friends and occasionally I visited him in his quarters, which was a huge privilege for a nursing student. We used to go to gospel meetings together. Then a Salvation Army doctor came from New Jersey, Dr. Herbert Rader, M.D. He too had had the same born again experience even though he was a Salvation Army captain. Through him I became involved in a campus prayer group where most of them had the same born-again experience. We were with hundreds of Salvation Army people, which made the association with these people very good for me.

Along with my spiritual growth things were going well academically for me too. I had been noticed by my superiors as a hard-working, smart student. When my second year test results came, Major Vera Williamson, the nursing superintendent from New Zealand, called all the second-year students to her office to announce our results. She said, "Everyone in your class passed except Ipe," and she paused for a few moments to look at everyone, including me.

I did not remember much after that because I felt that I was going to faint before she could complete the sentence. So many thoughts flashed through my mind. I thought of Dr. Macaden telling me that I was on my own. I thought about the fact that I had been a runaway. What would I do without this training? Would I be back in the street? I wondered what others would think of me. I had enjoyed the respect of my peers. Everyone thought I was smart, now that-and the influence it gave me- was coming to an end. I was profusely sweating, my head was reeling, and I was nauseated. I felt that I was about to fall. All this rushed in within a few moments; the time it takes to draw a breath...I held mine.

She finished her sentence, "... who received distinctions in the school." I was a top honors student that year out of a class of approximately 140 students. The shock was so much that some of my friends had to help me get out of that room.

With my third and final year, came more confidence and respect among my peers. I was elected as the president of the student council. As such I had to chair all the meetings to give guidance and leadership regarding affairs related to the student body. This was an honor. During that time Mrs. Kuruvilla joined her husband and accepted me as their best family friend. She was a great help and support. When I completed my third year I had the highest grade of any of my classmates despite only barely passing the practical portion of the exam.

Once I had finished my three-year course I had to return to the Swiss Emmaus team. They had started a new project earlier in Dharwar, Mysore. Dr. Macaden was the project leader. He had been waiting for me to finish my nursing because he wanted me to come back and set up a nursing department at Dharwar for the new hospital in Hubli. Due to his urgent need for my help he could not allow me to have any vacation even after my three hard years and nursing school. So I packed my things and headed back.

Chapter 5

A Sudden Change in Focus – losing eye sight

Without any hesitation I proceeded from Nagercoil on the first of July 1971 to Dharwar which was a three day journey. I had decided to travel by bus all the way so I would become familiar with the places. After staying a couple of days at home with my parents I continued my journey, the next day while visiting my brother Joy, in Calicut. I felt a strange feeling in my right eye as if black particles were moving around inside my eye. It bothered me but I continued on my journey, anxious to get to work.

I reached to Dharwar on a Friday afternoon and I was invited to have lunch with Dr. Macaden that next day. On the way over to his home I could not see the sun properly because of the sensation of spinning and the pain in my right eye. While we were having our lunch I told him what was happening. Immediately I was rushed to the ophthalmology clinic in Hubli medical College. After a thorough examination, the professor of ophthalmology told me that the situation was dangerous and that I would need to have complete bed rest for a month without moving my head.

This news was really upsetting to all of us because I had come to Dharwar with ready to begin working on the new project. The Swiss Emmaus and Dr. Macaden had continued to pay my salary for three years while they waited for me to complete my nursing school training. All that had led to me working at this new project. But even before I could put in an hour of work I had to deal with this new sickness. Everyone was very willing to accommodate me. All I could do was lie in bed for one month hoping that I would get better. Instead my condition deteriorated very rapidly in my right eye slowly started losing sight.

When the first month ended the doctor advised me to stay in bed another month. During the second month I began to have a high fever of unknown origin. If was so high that I lost all my strength. Finally, I was admitted to the Hubli Medical College where I needed around-the-clock care. In the hospital they tested for many things but could not find the real cause of my illness.

Confrontation with God

One morning after attending to my needs, the attendant went to wash my clothes. I was still lying in bed but I do not know if I was unconscious or sleeping. When I awoke I began to see, as if in a vision, someone standing beside me. He asked me to look around and see who could help me in my present circumstances. Despite those who loved me, a steady job and good income, I had nothing that could help me. When I realized my helpless and hopeless state, I burst into tears and began to cry aloud.

The nurses and the doctors didn't know what was happening to me. They tried to find out and called Dr. Macaden. He quickly came to the hospital but no one could console or comfort me. I asked them to leave me alone; I just wanted to cry. I was in God's presence and when we are in the presence of the Lord we do not need anyone's help to rejoice.

After a while a great peace came in to my heart. I wiped away all of my tears. By now I was just skin and bones and so weak that I even needed help to set up. Although everyone knew something was going on inside of me, they did not know what it was. I surrendered my life to Christ and waited upon His will for my life. I had already received God's free gift of Salvation but now I was beginning to surrender my life fully to His will. Salvation is the gift of forgiveness of sin and freedom from its bondage. It is a new hope without condemnation. Surrender on the other hand is a total yielding to God's plan.

My first confrontation with the Lord Jesus was while I was crying from the bottom of my heart in that place. He heard my cry and comforted me. Just like when Paul met Jesus on the way to Damascus, the people with him saw the light, but Paul heard the voice of Jesus. No one can explain that sweet, loving voice. Once Paul heard the voices blindness was not a problem. He wanted to hear the voice again to get direction. Thus he had no problem listening to Ananias. Paul was ready to pray and later to be baptized in water.

Many may see the light but they cannot hear the voice, the sweet voice of Jesus. Even among his ministers, some preached, some served at the tables, some ate bread, some fellowshipped, yet only a few heard the voice. Those who heard the voice did not mind the difficulties in serving God. The experience Paul had when he confronted Christ changed him from Saul to Paul, the greatest apostle to ever live.

Immediately after that loud cry, God's presence made me forget all my sorrows. I wiped away my tears, the fear vanished, and a new courage came into my heart. No matter what was to happen, I had the great assurance that I was his and he was mine. Later I would learn this moment was God selecting me to be a chosen vessel to carry the gospel of

Jesus Christ to the Gentiles, their kings, and people of many nations.

Despite that powerful moment, I continue to be sick in the hospital. The doctors were unable to diagnose my illness but they thought I had tuberculosis or a liver abscess. They tried various remedies but none had any effect on my illness. Concerned, Dr. Macaden sent a telegram to my home regarding my condition. My father and my brother, Raju, took the two-day journey to come see me. After spending a few days with me in the hospital, they decided to take me back to my apartment. My father had to return home but Raju stayed and cared for me almost another month. I was still having high fevers from the undiagnosed sickness. During that time my sisters and a group of other people kept praying for me, and the word assured them that I would not die of that illness. They kept writing to me and asking me to come home.

Finally, after two months of the high fever, Raju and I decided to pack up and leave Dharwar. The next day on the train ride back home, I laid down the entire trip. It took us two days to get home and as soon as I arrived I almost passed out. My family was surprised by my appearance. I looked like a long-haired skeleton draped in loose skin and I still could not sit up by my own strength.

Experiencing divine healing

The day I returned home to Pandalam, I had a small homemade meal. The next morning my sister said that we were going to fast and pray. She informed me that two great men of God were coming to pray with me. I had never heard of them but was eager for God to work in my life. Their names were Varyapuram Yohannan and Koodalil Kunjhu Kunju. Brother Yohannan came and sat down to pray and within a few minutes he diagnosed the illness I had and

began to prescribe medicines for each one of them. He had no medical knowledge but these were Holy Spirit filled men who were operating under the Gifts of the Spirit. *1 Corinthians 12:4-11 "There are different kinds of gifts but same spirits………………… All these are the work of one and the same Spirit……."*
These illnesses were not of a normal origin, but they were brought on by the effects of demonic spirits that wanted to attack my body and mind. These Spirits were part of generational curses and the effects of these curses. Most of what these men were saying I could not understand. When one would say that he saw something the other would say something related to that. Then they asked me some questions. They both spoke for a while in unknown tongues as they began to rebuke each one of the diseases.

In medicine, once a disease is diagnosed Doctors can begin to prescribe treatments to destroy the disease at the root. Physicians may find a particular bacteria or virus causing the sickness then they select a chemical component to kill the bacteria. These men of God used a different prescription. For each sickness they prescribe the same medicine: the name of Jesus. Because with this name that is above all other names, every knee shall bow, and every tongue will confess that Jesus is Lord.

Phil 2:9-11 " Therefore God exalted him to the highest place…….. Jesus Christ is Lord to the glory of God the Father."

Brother Yohannan said, "In the name of Jesus every sickness the doctors could not diagnose should leave this body." From then on, the sickness began to leave my body. There were neither scars nor residual traces from the illnesses. I had never before felt so good and free. After being sick for more than 2 months, two weeks of that spent in the hospital, it took only two hours in the presence of God to receive my miracle of healing. The greatest thing was that not only were those conditions healed but other problems I'd suffered with for years were healed that afternoon as well. After the morning prayer meeting I felt free.

Holy Spirit baptism

By that afternoon, I was already walking around. It felt good to exercise my healing in the presence of everyone. Then he said, "You are healed from your sicknesses but you need to be filled with the Holy Spirit." I wanted to be filled with the Holy Spirit but I wondered how God could give His spirit to an unworthy person like me? In the evening meeting I began to be able to move my whole body. Remember I had been bedridden for nearly two months so the fact that I could move my head, neck, arms, and legs was miraculous. Before my healing I had to be cautious, a sudden movement could have cost me my sight. Once when my boss took me to the doctor and his car he had to go between 10 and 15 mph because if I shook my head it was possible that I would lose my sight.

When the Spirit of God began to move in my heart, my body began to shake. New strength started moving into my body. I started dancing in the Spirit. I was thrown from one side of the room to the other. The fear of shaking my head vanished. Then I cried out and said several times "I surrender all, I surrender all, I surrender all!" Suddenly I began to speak in a way I never had before. I was speaking in tongues, though there were only a few words. That night I could not sleep, I was continuously praying and speaking in this new found language. That brought new strength, courage, and power.

The name of Jesus and the power of the Holy Spirit brought a new sense of direction, authority, and power to my life. I finally felt that I was in control of my life. When there was a problem or sickness, I could take charge of it through the power of God. I could pray for deliverance or rebuke it in the name of Jesus. I realized it was not the size of the problem that mattered, but in whose name I was standing and fighting the enemy. The new experience of getting filled in Holy Spirit and speaking in unknown tongues gave me a spiritual victory and authority over demonic forces, sickness, and problems.

Returning to work

Within a few days I regained all the strength I'd lost and I decided it was time to go back to work in Dharwar. Since I had been sick for such a long time, I decided to have someone help me. I thought it would be best to take an unemployed neighbor boy with me to help out and also to find him a job. We both left for Dharwar and we shared the apartment I had lived in before. I provided food and lodging and he cooked for us while I was gone. I shared everything I had with him.

My fast return to Dharwar surprised everyone, including my bosses who were doctors. They never thought that I would regain strength or get well so soon. I took less than a week off before I began to work full time sometimes I work 12 hours a day, which I'd never done since I went to Dharwar.

Of all the ailments I'd had when I left Dharwar, I returned with only some pain and vision loss in my right eye. The doctors insisted I take medicines, even though they were never able to accurately diagnose my problem. I continued working despite the headaches, pain, and sensitivity to light because I didn't want to disappoint the people who'd done so much for me. I coped by keeping my right eye closed as much as possible.

I was also adjusting to an area that had a new climate and set of customs that I was unfamiliar with. A newly spiritual person must have some fellowship, but there were no Spirit-filled Christians or Churches that I knew of in the area. I did find a group of Christians in the area, a newly started Brethren assembly, which include a small group of people. They were very nice to me but they were not at all familiar with the spiritual experience I'd encountered. Since I did not know much about in depth Christian life, I lived the best way I knew how and sought fellowship with others whenever I could.

One day I returned home from work to find the locked cabinet where I stored my money stolen. I looked through my apartment to find that not only was my money gone but so were my clothes and the neighbor boy I'd brought with me. It didn't take long to realize that he'd robbed me and taken nearly all of my possessions with him. I didn't have time to worry about it though because my eyesight was becoming a greater concern to everyone, especially to the Swiss Emmaus. They had invested quite a bit in me, my education, and my medical expenses. They wondered if I would ever get better.

I was sent to different medical colleges and to many well-known physicians and ophthalmologists. I was sent to professor of ophthalmology at Hubli medical center and treated at the Christian Medical College in Vellore, one of the leading hospitals in India. In addition I was sent to Bangalore Medical College and Bangalore Cantonment Hospital. I spent two to three weeks at each of these hospitals under-going numerous tests, investigations, and observations. I had at different times, spinal taps, dilation of my pupils, corneal injection, a patch placed on my eye, drops, ointments, and injections but the only outcome was total blindness. I was left with a painful and very uncomfortable situation without any cure. Finally, the professor of ophthalmology, at Vellore CMC Hospital, told me that I was lucky that I had one good eye. There was nothing more they could do. I left there with total loss of vision in my right eye.

The only thing I had in my life at that time was the fullness of peace that passed all understanding. I did not worry much about what would happen to me in my life, though there were plenty of things to be worried about. Being very independent from childhood, nobody was there to feel sorry for me. There was no one really to count on, including my parents, because of the way I'd lived my life up to that point. I worked and earned more money than anyone else at home and spent all of it as I wished. So it was not easy to go back and live as a dependent of my parents or anyone else.

Additionally, a 27 year old blind man would not be welcomed to marry into a decent family, or even to marry a good-looking girl. I had proved my ability to excel in my chose profession but what good would that do me if I didn't have good eyesight. The last thing I wanted was to be a burden on anyone but looking in to my future all I saw was darkness and hopelessness. Despite the gloomy possibilities, these things were not bothering me because I knew the Lord was in control of my life

God's willingness to help me became clear one morning when I had a vision. In the vision, Jesus appeared to me. Then I saw the construction of a building with stones. The foundation was already laid and He had selected me as the cornerstone. My knowledge of the visions was very limited. I did not understand anything clearly. I didn't do anything good to please God or to deserve such assurances of my future. The only thing I could remember was that I never had complained about what I was going through nor had I ever ask God why he had chosen me to go through these situations.

Worse before they're better

One day I was having lunch at Dr. Macaden's house. Suddenly I felt something rushing in to my eye. They rushed me to Bangalore Contonment Hospital, and then to Bangalore Medical College Hospital. I underwent another series of tests, including spinal taps. During that time Dr. Harris of England was doing research in Bangalore and I became his private patient. Despite everything he checked he could not find the real cause of my blindness. He then referred me to a group of physicians at Bangalore Medical College.

Finally, the medical team at Bangalore medical College came up with a diagnosis. They theorized that I was allergic to the tuberculosis bacteria, which caused a vitreous hemorrhage inside my eye resulting in blindness. This finding was accepted, though very controversial because it was a hypothesis more than a diagnosis. I had been working among leprosy patients whose disease was caused by Mycobacterium Leprae, which is also found in the same family of the tuberculosis bacteria. In any case, I came back and had to continue being treated, without any effect. Everyone began to accept the fact that I was a sick person since no one really saw me well.

Healing of a blind eye

At a Sunday evening prayer meeting at church a sister who taught at one of the local universities stood up to pray. She said "Lord, ever since Ipe came to this place he has been sick; it seems there is no way out of it. Please Lord do help him." She was very sincere in her prayers.

I heard that prayer and began to feel pity for myself for the first time. I prayed "Lord, if you want me to be half-blind, please tell me Lord. If not, please give me my sight now." I thanked God and told Him I was open to His will. When

I left that prayer meeting it was beginning to get dark. As I walked to my apartment I suddenly saw something strange. A truck was coming down the road in the opposite direction with the headlights on. I could see it. Then I realized I saw it with my blind eye. Seeing with my blind eye was like seeing lightening in the sky. For the first time in almost eight months I saw light with my right eye. It was incredible that God had heard me so fast after suffering all those months with various tests.

The next morning I decided to walk the two miles to work with my left eye closed. Since the left eye was the only one that had good vision it was difficult, but as I continued to keep the left eye closed, my right eye improved. I did this for two or three days and my site continued to improve until I could see the road with my right eye. Within two weeks I began to read the New Testament, the smaller edition, with my right eye. That was the end of the blindness I'd been suffering from for months. I once was blind but now I could see.

When I began to get my vision back new hope and joy began to flood into my life. Prayers were being answered instantaneously. The feeling of defeat that had picked at me vanished and I walked in victory. Hopelessness was replaced with hope, confidence, courage and purpose. People no longer needed to feel sympathy for me and I did not have to depend upon the mercy of others. I was able to do things for myself just like any other person.

This great deliverance was visible to everyone around me, especially those who knew me. They were all happy for me, and I once again found purpose in my adulthood.

Standing for my faith

I gradually began to work more and also got bolder and stronger in my faith in God. I began to share my personal experiences with many who are in my office. They had no problem accepting me but they were sensing a dangerous situation. As I have mentioned before, the organization I was working for was based out of Switzerland which meant it was a secular European one that did things for humanitarian reasons. The locals were very strong Hindus and strongly anti-Christian. If any of them knew I was propagating Christianity, Swiss Emmaus would have had a lot of opposition. Therefore, my boss was really very concerned about my activities, especially my witnessing and testifying to others. They liked and cared for me but they needed to be mindful of their own jobs.

I was excited to help the community in any way I could so during the Christmas of 1971 I joined a group of Christian workers who came to that area. Along with local believers, they decide to visit houses in many villages. We went in small groups and visited approximately 150 villages in that area. We distributed Christian literature, Gospels, and witnessed to the people. I was with them the entire time. I didn't realize the problem my actions could have caused until I went back to work.

Because of this activity many people in the villages recognized me. They began to connect my Christian work after hours with my job with Swiss Emmaus. Since the villagers identified me as a Christian worker, the so-called nonreligious social organization could not prove to them that they were not religious.

My boss decided to confront me and he gave me an option. If I were to continue with them I would refrain from involving myself with any Christian outreach activities. I would also have to refrain from letting others know I was a Christian. Otherwise, I would have to quit my job. It was a very hard decision to make. This job was the only dignified thing I had accomplished in my life up to that point. My entire life was committed to the job. I loved not only the job but the people I worked with. It was a noble cause that allowed me to serve the most needy.

In the natural, if I lost that job, it would be very hard to find another. I had invested ten years of my life to that job and, because of my seniority, I was making good money, serving the most needy. I was very proud of it and of course they paid me a good salary.

There was also the issue of my illness. Even though I had sight in my left eye, I was considered disabled. That meant it wasn't wise to enter into any new jobs.

I also felt I needed to be faithful to the institution that gave me the opportunity to accomplish something when others saw no value in me. Swiss Emmaus, and their staff, had invested so much of their time and money in my education and also my medical treatment. They had accepted my disability without any complaints or regrets.

Beyond everything else, they trusted me with responsibilities, and did not treat me like just another worker, but as an equal so that I could be a part of the management team. I was one of the most trusted members of the team and my name was well known amongst the Swiss Emmaus organization.

I really did not want to disappoint them. I was in a dilemma. I could not question their decision and I knew it would be foolish to leave my job. It would mean throwing away my career after a decade of work and study.

When all of that was weighed against my faith the choice was clear. I could not deny my faith.

It was God who gave me the courage and boldness to tell the boss that I could not deny my faith in God at any cost to achieve anything in this world. Because of nursing school and eight months of sickness I had very little to carry me until I could find a new job, and the Swiss Emmaus didn't have any other positions they could give me. I was back to square one again. I could not blame my boss for their decision. It had been made with their headquarters.

Finally one of the hospitals affiliated with the Swiss Emmaus at Kumbakonam, Tamil Nadu, agreed to hire me as a staff nurse for less than half the salary I was getting in my current position. The only choice left for me was to accept this job or deny my faith in God in order to stay where I had been making a good salary and holding a high position. I made the right choice.

Chapter 6

Getting Married

In March of 1972, I left Dharwar, Hubli and went home for a short break before going on to my next job. When I came home, my parents suggested that I get married. I was 28 years old at the time and I thought that this next step would be a good idea.

Then, as now, arranged marriage was a common custom in India. It is a very long process, full of tradition. Normally, the parents of the bride or groom do the matchmaking for their children. The selection is based on religion, race or sect, family status, education or professional status, and appearance of the person. Then the family arranges for one to go to the other's house. Usually it is the man who will go to the home of the woman; there he will see her in the presence of several people. Then they decide if they'd like to go on with that proposal. In the olden days there was a dowry system where there was a lump sum of money given by the woman's family, to the man's family. This was considered her share of her parent's wealth, but this is no longer done.

Normally if both agree there will be a formal engagement ceremony. There is no unsupervised dating or time alone before a formal engagement. Issues of compatibility are worked out during the marriage. Individuals enter into the marriage by faith, trusting in God that everything will work out well.

Before I arrived home from Dharwar my parents had a proposal in hand. They did the initial matchmaking and it was up to me to decide if I would go along with it. Since I only had a few days before I had to report to my new job, I had to do things much faster.

I selected a day to go meet Susie and I had a friend from church join me. Susie's was a middle-class family that lived at the top of a steep hill. The pathway up was long. I struggled up the hill in a Dhoti, careful to hold it up as I walked. I'm sure they were enjoying the amusing show.

When we arrived there were many people in the house for the event. There were elders from their local church, many close family members, as well as her immediate family. It was a very formal event.

I didn't want to put on a big show, and opted to wear a Dhoti rather than my usual pants and shirt. With my short hair, tall, thin frame, and fresh shave, I imagine I must have looked like a local peasant.

A couple of days prior to my visit to their home, God had shown me a vision of a girl who I knew from my school days. She was one of the darkest people I had come across among the Indians. In the vision, I was also asked if I would have any problem marrying this girl if it were God's will. I told the Lord that if it was His will that I should marry her, I would not object.

No one who knew me thought I would have an arranged marriage of my parent's choice. By that time, I had been away from home for 12 years and had lived my life independently. However, I had surrendered my life completely to God, and that included the selection of a wife for me. My only desire in my heart was to follow the will of God. I had given up trying to do it all myself because I was a total failure on my own.

When I arrived at Susie's house my friend and I were invited to sit down for coffee. Unmarried girls do not come and sit with elderly men, only married women may, therefore Susie was not with us.

We continued talking but Susie had not been invited out to meet us. Single girls are often times quite shy, especially when someone comes to meet them in the presence of their family. My friend asked them if we could see Susie and a short while later she came out and served us some homemade desserts and coffee. She came out onto the veranda, in front of the people gathered there. I thought that she was very beautiful from the moment I saw her. I didn't need to ask any more questions about her. I knew my answer. Then I was allowed to talk to her for a few minutes privately.

Susie was brought up as a God-fearing Christian girl. She served diligently in her church and demonstrated a strong faith in God wherever she went. She had had a very different life from mine. She was a quiet girl with a calm, decent manner. I was concerned that her Brethren up brining meant she wasn't familiar with the baptism of the Holy Spirit, or even miracles, despite their strong emphasis on the Word of God.

I let her know my life was different from a lot of other people because I did not worry about what others thought of me. I sought God's approval.

We chatted a little while longer. Susie was a professional nurse who had worked in India and Bahrain for years. At that time she was on her annual leave before returning to a new and better job.

After having a few minutes to talk together alone, we returned. I liked her very much, but I wanted to see the will of God in this matter. We went to a prophet of God who we had known for a long time. His name was Varyapuram

Yohannan. He confirmed in the spirit that it was God's will that the marriage take place within a few days.

Shortly after the engagement was announced I was in her town to invite one of our relatives who knew Susie's family. While there I saw Susie and her sister shopping in town. Although we had seen each other, neither one of us approached the other. She was shy as I was.

In those days the engagement function was still a family event. Usually the host family will invite all their family, friend, and neighbors for a dinner. Since her family hosted the event it is likely Susie was there, however, I was not. This was not unusual for that time, although now both bride and groom attend these events.

During the large dinner a date for the marriage is announced and there is a time of celebration. Today, since both parties attend, there are often prayers given by pastors of the churches, testimonies given, stories of their first meeting shared, and even entertainment.

At the engagement party it was decided that our wedding would take place April 17, 1972. We invited all of our relatives, friends, acquaintances, church members, pastors and leaders in the church and community.

I chose to wear a three-piece suit in my wedding, even though it was 95 degrees without Air conditioning. Despite the fact that such western items are common now, I may have been one of the first to wear a suit in my town. Susie wore a very fine, white, traditional Indian Sari. She looked very beautiful. Our wedding ceremony was at my home church, the Pandalam-The Church of God in India. It was special to me because my family was among the founding members of the church. The late pastor T.M. Varghese, a well-known pastor and overseer of the Church of God in India, solemnized our wedding. The ceremony lasted almost 3 1/2 hours. Many pastors preached from the Word of God for hours. I wasn't sure I'd be ready to undertake such a divine responsibility, given my old life, but God strengthened both of us and it was a blessed ceremony.

Ours was considered a modified arranged marriage. The typical Indian custom is to have the wedding and then spend days and nights at the homes of various members of the family. The bride and groom are invited to stay as a guest for several days at each home which means the wedding celebration can drag on for days. Sometimes after this the couple will go away for a honeymoon, or this time with family is considered the honeymoon.

We skipped many of these formalities and instead left a couple of days after the wedding ceremony for our honeymoon in Kanyakumari, the southernmost part of India where the Indian Ocean, Arabian Sea, and the Bay of Bengal join in one place.

It was a beautiful place to watch the sunrise and sunset. Then, after only 10 days of being married, I had to leave to start my new job at Kumbakonam in Tamilnadu.

New job and experiences in Kumbakonam

The Sacred Heart Hospital of Kumbakonam was a Catholic hospital run by the Sisters of Charity. It was a large leprosy Hospital, highly organized with a large staff. I was just one among many and was assigned an ordinary job. After years with the Swiss Emmaus, I was not used to this. Despite my demotion, all the people there were very considerate of me, and whenever possible accommodated me in their quarters and brought food to me from the convent.

Susie decided to join me there. So, after a couple of months, she came and joined me at Kumbakonam. Unfortunately, despite having a job, we could not get a decent house to live in. We went to one of the main streets and found a little one room hut. It was to be our first home as a married couple. Even though we both had had very comfortable homes, we lived in that little hut among the other villagers who spoke different languages. During this time we joined one of the local Tamil churches and had very good fellowship with them.

Our life at Kumbakonam is memorable as that was the beginning of our family life. After many years of living an arrogant bachelor's life, I was learning to settle down. Even though we lived in a hut, people really respected and loved us. God worked so wonderfully, as we were at work, in church, or even on the street.

One day one of the brothers brought us a live duck as a gift. Susie prepared a very nice duck curry in the special Kerala way. As we were getting ready to eat lunch on that Saturday afternoon, someone knocked at our door.

It was a beggar asking for food. Immediately I took a quarter rupee and gave it to him. He very happily walked away because people usually only give five or ten paisa. Suddenly I heard a voice in my heart say, "The man asked for food and you gave him money instead of food."

The food was ready for us to eat. I told Susie what I had heard. She asked me to look for that man. As I looked outside, a sudden rainstorm came and began to pour down heavily. I took an umbrella and began to follow him, but I could not see him on the road since it was raining so heavily.

At last I found him, standing by the side of a shop keeping himself away from the heavy downpour. I approach the beggar and asked him to come back to our house for some food. So we shared our food with him. We served him first and, after he left, we had our lunch. That was one of the tastiest meals we ever had in our life.

We didn't see what we had done as unusual; it was a way of life. Even though we did not have much, we were happy to share what we did have with those who had even less. This and many other wonderful experiences became the foundation of our family life.

A time of transition

We had a number of mini-adventures, good and bad, that formed the early years of our marriage. While we were living in the hut we were allowed to use the toilet in the landlord's house. One day he got angry, though we didn't know why, and closed the gate on us. So we had to use paper bags for our waste and then get on a bicycle and throw it away. We didn't allow ourselves to become too discouraged with this change.

One night a group of rowdy drunks came to attack us with knives. I had to stand and face them in the middle of the night. The mighty hand of God worked on our behalf because one of our local friends came immediately to my rescue with some others and the gang disbursed. That same night we moved out of that hut. Immediately I called the hospital and they sent their van to pick us up. The people at the Sacred Heart Hospital and the mother superior were very nice to us.

Another day the hospital chaplain, a Catholic priest, told me that in his absence I could minister to the patients in the hospital by giving last rites. That was something new for me and it gave me a chance to share and pray with patients and staff.

Our time in Kumbakonam was constantly changing. Sometimes we lived in nice European accommodations were the Anglo staff stayed, and other times we lived in a small hut with the villagers. This was the time I began seeing and experience the divine healing of God in others. God was actually working through me. I had experienced healing, but now God was using me to bring healing to others.

Ministering to needs

One day Susie and I were invited to dinner in the home of one of our fellow church members. When we arrived there we saw that the father of the House was bedridden due to a high fever. He was wrapped up in blankets and could not even get up. He asked me to pray for him. As a new Christian, I felt uneasy about laying my hands on the elderly man, yet I touched his shoulder and prayed. God healed him immediately and he got up and served us. In fact, he even joined us for dinner.

That night I met with a couple who were relatives of the family. They were well educated and worked in north India. The wife of a Catholic from Tamil Nadu and the husband was a Hindu and communist activists from Kerala. The wife said to me, "I have been trying to take my husband to the Catholic Church for 15 years, but have never succeeded."

That evening I talked to him and shared the Word of God. He was very accepting of the experiences I had had with Christ and that night he repented of his sins and got saved. Almost immediately I could see a true conversion in that man. At the time I did not realize that God was using me as a vessel to win souls for the Kingdom and bring his healing to others.

One of the greatest miracles

One day in a clinical staff meeting the chief medical officer came and mentioned a patient whom I had not yet seen. His name was Arumugam, and he was a professional accountant. He had a young wife and two young children, around three and five years old. Mr. Arumugam was quite sick and was very close to death. The doctors told him that he was going to die within a week, so they asked the family to make arrangements for the funeral. He was being kept alive with high doses of steroids, 480 mg of prednisone a day. The spirit of the Lord put a desire in my heart to visit him in his room.

I walked in that evening, not sure what I would see. In front of me was a man in great agony. Sores covered his bloated body and he was in so much pain he could not even sit up on his bed. He had been diagnosed with *lepromatous leprosy with an acute reaction*. It was a very painful and inflammatory ulcerative condition. I had no words to console him. In my almost 10 years with leprosy patients, I had not seen anyone like him before.

As soon as I entered his room he opened his eyes and looked at my face. His eyes searched mine for some hint of hope, or even mercy. With his condition, he did not have anything to say or to look forward to. I told him that I knew a physician who had helped me and who would help him too. I immediately had his attention. I explained the loving kindness of Jesus to him. Then I shared my experience of sickness and blindness and how this doctor had healed me.

His eyes got wider and filled with tears. He looked at my face with so much hope as I told him the doctor's name. I said, "His name is Jesus Christ." I continued sharing my testimony for a few more minutes. I explained how Jesus had taken care of my infirmities when there was no hope. I could see Mr. Arumugam was already beginning to feel different and he began to pay keen attention to know this God I was talking about. Being a Hindu Brahmin, which meant a high class Hindu, this was all new information to him.

Before leaving his room I gave him the New Testament that I had always carried with me. I left for home that evening. The next day when I came into work I first went to Mr.Arumugam's room to see if he had made it through the night. As soon as I got into his room, he opened his eyes and looked at me saying, "Sir, I did not sleep all night. I was reading the New Testament you gave me. I want to know more about this Jesus Christ."

I spent a few minutes talking to him about the saving grace of God and his son Jesus Christ. In the middle of a conversation he asked me how he could receive this Jesus into his life. We closed our eyes and I led him in the sinner's prayer. He repeated every word I said. I could see a big change on his face. He looked at me, and said,

"I have never felt like this before."

Getting ready to come to America

While I was in Kumbakonam I corresponded with the American consulate in Madras about getting a visa to go to America. I was trying to register with the state Board of Nursing in the state of New York. Dr. and Mrs. Kuruvilla, whom I'd met many years prior when I was in nursing school, were helping me. Dr.Kuruvilla was doing his residency in New York at the time.

I was still working at the hospital but I had only been given a nine month long assignment. The pay had been barely enough for us to survive on, but now Susie was expecting our first child. I was facing the prospect of no job at the same time as the birth of our new child. Since the prospects of finding work that would pay all of our bills were dismal, I set my sights to going to America.

Before going to Madras for my immigration interview, I went to say goodbye to Arumugam

The next day I boarded the train to Madras. I spent the day at the US Consulate with the medical officer. A medical check is required to receive a visa to the US so he examined me thoroughly. He repeatedly checked my eyes to make sure everything was normal. He had a suspicious look on his face as he dilated my pupils to examine them a second time.

Finally he said, "I cannot find anything wrong." And gave me the letter saying I was physically fit.

I reflected on all the infirmities I had suffered in the last year and how the Lord Almighty had completely healed me of everything. I delivered the papers to US Consulate the next morning. They looked at the papers and asked me to come back in the evening to get my visa.

I went from the US Consulate to the Bible Society to purchase a Tamil Bible for Arumugam. That night I sent a telegram to Dr. Macaden asking them to officially release me from my duties under the Swiss Emmaus Association. I had to travel all night back to Kumbakonam from Madras. I only had one more week to complete my contract of nine months with the Sacred Heart Hospital at Kumbakonam.

I went to see Mr. Arumugam the day I came back from Madras. He told me that he felt a lot better and that his sores were healing quickly. He felt stronger and wanted to go home. I was thrilled when his doctor said he could go home the next day.

After spending four months in the hospital, the doctor had told him that he would not live another week. But, in less than five days time, he was healed and everyone was amazed by his quick recovery. His healing began when he heard the name of Jesus for the first time. Only by hearing the name of Jesus Mr. Arumugam, who had been left to die, received complete healing. The next morning he was discharged from the hospital and walked to my apartment to get the Tamil Bible I had bought for him. He was back to Pondichery, his hometown. After 10 years of being in the medical field I had not seen any such recovery. And now after 38 years, that was one of the greatest miracles I've ever seen. I am still astonished by the way God works miracles.

Chapter 7

Leaving Kumbakonam to go to the USA

The next day, I went to see the Mother Superior of the hospital. She was very surprised to hear that I had applied and received a visa to go to America. That seemed strange to me since she should have seen all the paperwork coming and going. Nonetheless, she released me from all my duties one week early. I left Kumbakonam and went to Kerala with Susie who was full-term with our first child. It was a one and a half day train ride to get to our hometown for the birth of our first child.

As was the custom, the first delivery was taken care of by Susie's parents in their home. Therefore, when we arrived in Pandalam Susie's family came and brought me customary gifts, then took Susie immediately to her family's home in Aranmula.

A few days after Susie left I was feeling very sick, vomiting continuously, I began losing weight and I was jaundice. I realized these were the symptoms Hepatitis-B.

Before leaving Kumbakonam I was taking care of lots of patients with Hepatitis–B at the hospital. I went to see a physician and he confirmed my fear.

I didn't know what to do. I had infectious hepatitis but they did not have any specific treatment for it. He could only treat my symptoms, but not the disease. I was getting progressively worse. Despite having my immigrant visa to travel to the US, I would no longer be able to travel because of the Hepatitis. I continued to travel between Pandalam and Aranmula for a few days until I became too sick to travel at all.

We tried to see joy despite this latest infirmity but I grew sicker. Finally I was too sick to spend time with my wife especially during those final, difficult days of pregnancy. Everybody predicted that we would have a son. As long as it was a healthy baby it did not matter if it was a boy or a girl to us. Since I had a wretched life, I prayed several times, "God, please don't give our children my character."

On the morning of February 17, 1973, our daughter Elizabeth was born. I could not be with my wife during her labor because I was very sick, and at that time we did not have phones, so I sent my brother for news. He visited the hospital and brought the news of the arrival of our baby girl. That evening, somehow, I went and saw them in the hospital. When I saw Elizabeth I realized that my prayers were heard and answered by God. Not only was Elizabeth beautiful just like Susie, I could tell she was very gentle and had a good character.

Visit of a very special person

At the end of February 1973 many believers gathered together in my home to pray for me. That evening, after prayer while all the believers were standing on our veranda, a car stopped in front of our house and two people came to our home. My father recognized one of them as Pastor P.J. Daniel of Mavelikara and the other was Pastor John Osteen, an American pastor from Texas. Since I was very much acquainted with the Europeans and people of other nationalities, I conversed with them. Pastor Osteen prayed for my healing and that night I was miraculously healed of hepatitis.

The very next week I felt much better and I started making plans for my trip to the USA. On March 28, 1973, I left India leaving my wife and our six week old baby at home.

My trip to America had a few stops. The plane stopped in Kuwait, Athens, then Zürich, and England. In England I stayed one night in a transit hotel and the next day I continued my journey to New York's JFK airport. It was an exciting time as I looked forward to the things ahead. In those days, people were allowed to leave India with very little money. I had only eight dollars. I made the decision to spend two dollars of that money on headphones so that I could listen to music. Perhaps that was not the wisest decision for someone in my place, but I can now say that God blessed me from my six dollar beginning.

New life in New York

I reached New York on April 4, 1973. My friend, Dr. Kuruvilla, and a Salvation Army officer came to receive me. We had dinner at his house and I stayed in a one-bedroom apartment on Colden Street in Flushing with Dr. and Mrs. Kuruvilla. They were very kind and generous to allow me to stay with them. We all shared the housework and expenses. Before even looking for a job, I began looking for a church to worship at. The first Sunday, I went with Dr. and Mrs. Kuruvilla to a Baptist church. I had a nice time but as a Pentecostal believer, I was looking for a Pentecostal church.

The following Saturday I walked around and found a church about 5 miles away. It was an Assembly of God church in Flushing. The Assembly of God churches worship in the Holy Spirit and pray in tongues so I could relate more to that service. I enjoyed the first service there and, with time, I became a member.

The pastor was Reverend Gunnar Jacobson, a very nice, hard-working pastor. They had a special group of believers in the church who were hippies. In the early 1970s there were a lot of hippies in New York and its suburbs. Pastor Jacobson had a special heart for these perishing young men and women, most of whom were drug addicts. He gathered volunteers to go to the hippie camps to witness to them and bring them to the church. When I first joined there I met with many of these very zealous, young people with long hair and long beards. Some of them became my friends. Among them was David Penchesky a young, Jewish, ex-hippie. He was anointed with the Holy Spirit and ministered to people. I had several chances to go with them on this particular outreach.

The church also had a very strong men's ministry of which I was a part. We witnessed in subway stations, on street corners and went house to house to evangelize. I enjoyed reaching out to these different people without hesitation. Later, David Penchesky became Dean of the Bible School in that church and I was able to take several courses in biblical studies.

Meanwhile, I joined the Booth Memorial medical center as a staff graduate nurse working the night shift. In order to continue my work I needed to pass the Board tests. So I worked at night and studied in the library during the day. When I asked about the material on the test I learned that there would be two subject areas I had not studied in India: obstetrics and gynecology and psychiatric nursing. I had no understanding of either of these subjects and I could not go back to school because I had a job. That meant I would need to study these tests on my own.

Before the first State Board Examination I went to the library to study. I prayed, "Lord, I can only take some reference books and try to study on my own. If I do not pass Obstetrics and Gynecology I will never be able to practice here." Even though I was a top student in my class, I had a hard time. However, on the first test, I passed three subjects, including Obstetrics and Gynecology. Therefore, I was able to begin working with my temporary license.

Then came the second State Board Examination. During that time there was rampant cheating with most of the foreign graduates purchasing copies of the test and memorizing the answers. I had not cheated, nor had I passed. I was beginning to feel a great deal of pressure. If I did not pass the examination when I took it again, I would not be able to continue as a graduate nurse anymore. Most of the foreigners had passed their exams and therefore, there was no scarcity of nurses. I continued to study the remaining two subjects while working on my temporary permit.

Since the government knew that the previous examination papers had gotten out, they made the next test much harder than before. My supervisor told me that because my temporary license would expire soon I must get my license in order to remain in my present job. That night I went home and prayed, "Lord, you know what I'm going through." Then I went to take the exam. Only three foreign graduates passed that State Board Examination in New York City, although thousands took the exam. I was one of the three who passed. And I did it with high marks.

The start of a young family

After nine months in America, my wife Susie and our little 11-month-old daughter, Elizabeth, came from India and we moved into a new apartment. Even though we had a wonderful time before I left India, everything was new now. A mother, a small baby, a new environment, night shifts, studies, a job and no one else around to do things for us. We had to do everything on our own.

Life was not easy for Susie or me. She had to adjust to the new environment where she had no friends, relatives, or loved ones. She had a hard time in that new situation. Maybe my lack of understanding was part of the reason for the rough time, yet I was comfortable. I liked my job and the people with whom I worked. I had to work hard and work overtime to make ends meet. Although Susie was a nurse, and was trying for her license, I did not help the way she expected me to. During this time, Susie stayed home as a housewife while I worked in the hospital working both regular hours and overtime.

Despite our hardships during this time, we were able to help many. We had the typical life of new immigrants in New York. Everything was fascinating. We rode the subways, visited the Statue of Liberty, and met different people. After seeing many parts of New York City, I thought all of America was built with concrete and iron.

On June 13, 1975, Susie gave birth to our son, Jacob. He brought even more happiness to our lives. He was an American citizen, a Yankee. As the family grew, so did the responsibilities. I was compelled to work more shifts than normal to stay ahead of the bills. We had social obligations with family friends. We celebrated birthdays, holidays and, anniversaries together, yet I felt as separated from the others. First of all, I was a born-again, Spirit-filled Christian who wanted to serve God. I had the desire to witness to others and get involved in the church. This took many of the social and cultural friends away from us.

As we continued living in New York, the signs of prosperity started to show up. We moved from our one-bedroom apartment to a two-bedroom apartment. Instead of public transportation; we were able to buy a used car; and we got to know many more people. We also began attending Malayalee churches occasionally. Malayalee churches are churches where the services are conducted in my native language.

The work at Booth Memorial Hospital was good. Even though there were hundreds of thousands of employees, both union and non-union, the administration noticed the sincere and hard work I was doing. They wrote about me in the hospital newsletter in appreciation of my service. This was a Salvation Army hospital and I, having been trained by the Salvation Army school of nursing in India, had been recommended by the officers there.

The experiences in New York were rather unique. Most of the time, we lived in high-rise buildings where anything we needed was readily available. There was no scarcity, but there was a growing concern for living in such tight surroundings. The population was constantly shifting, and the effects became very fearful for us. We always asked God to protect us from any evil that might come before us, and he did. And as the children were growing up we did not want them to be in such constrained surroundings. Shortly thereafter, we made plans to leave New York.

Chapter 8

Life in Houston

In 1975, I took a trip west to visit places outside of New York. I visited some old friends in Oklahoma City, Dallas, Houston, and Chicago. I liked the countryside and country living, so I started to have a desire to move out of New York City. Especially as new immigrants, the fast life in New York did not appeal to me as a place to raise a family. So we wanted to leave New York before our children were old enough to start school.

My first task was to learn the process. One day I was talking to a Keralite pastor who was also an insurance salesman. He had bought a house and was moving out of New York. I questioned him for hours about ways to buy a house in Houston, but he never gave me a straight answer. Although that upset me a little, God provided another contact. I went to Houston, met with the real estate agent, and saw many houses. On my first day in Houston I signed a contract for a beautiful house in a nice suburban community then flew home that same night. In May of 1978 we packed our bags, took a flight to Houston, and settled in our newly purchased house. Life in Houston started with new changes.

In addition to our desire to escape the city, we needed to leave New York for the sake of my wife, Susie's, health. She'd had a difficult time adjusting to the new environment. She could not adjust to the severe cold weather that brought on asthma attacks and weakness in her body. There were also emotional trials. She had to learn to be a mother and a house-wife. She had been a professional nurse in India. While she was able to work in Bahrain she made much more money than I ever made. She had also accomplished many things in her own right before we were ever married. These new changes made it hard for her.

Thus, when we moved to Houston into our own house, it was a nice change. In our first week in Houston she found a nursing job and began driving. She felt much better, but the Houston humidity did not give her much relief from asthma. At that time Houston was a booming city with many job opportunities. The oil industry was growing quickly and lots of people were moving to Houston at that time. I began to explore several opportunities instead of jumping at the first offer. Many pastors, including Keralite pastors, also moved to Houston and started many churches. As new immigrants came, churches began to grow with families seeking familiar affiliations.

When we first arrived in Houston we were contacted by a Keralite pastor and we began to go to their fellowship. Later that year another Keralite pastor and his family moved from Chicago to our neighborhood and we soon became friends with them. The pastor and I registered a church in Houston and it grew to be a good fellowship.

One day, a pastor from Dallas visited our church. After the service, he visited our home and prayed for Susie's asthma. She instantly received a full, miraculous healing from asthma and she's never had asthma again. This divine healing improved her body, mind, and spiritual life. Until then, I was the only one who had experienced a miraculous healing. But now my wife and family started experiencing God's power in their lives.

After looking at a few hospitals, I took a job in a local smaller, private hospital as the charge nurse. It was an entry-level management job where I was paid for 40 hours a week to work three, 12 hour shifts. I was in charge of 15 to 20 staff members and a ward. Overall, the atmosphere was very good. From the beginning it was a friendly, Christian oriented atmosphere. Even the director of nurses was a born-again Christian and many of the subordinates there had similar experiences.

Moving from New York to Houston's suburb had been a big change, but slowly we were able to adjust. In the beginning it was difficult for us. Having moved from a big city, known as "the city that never sleeps" to a smaller city and its suburbs we learn to live here without much problem and adjusted well to our surroundings.

At the end of 1978, I became an American citizen. It was a momentous day in my life. I started my life with no hope or future. From those humble beginnings, God established a spirit of hope in me, which was part of the foundation of this country. America was open to anyone and provided the opportunity to succeed. I thank God for His provisions and leading me here to expand my opportunities and to give my family a chance for a different, better future.

In 1979, we decided to visit our families back in India for the first time in 6 years. We spent a month in India and it was at that time I noted my mother's pitiful condition. She had been an asthma patient for a long time and the treatments she was taking caused her to have hypertension that went unnoticed. When the hypertension increased she had a stroke that paralyzed her on one side of her body. Her disability grew worse and eventually she fell and broke her hip. That resulted in her being bedridden. Since I'd been gone for so long, I did not realize her condition.

I decided to bring my whole family to America. I came back to the US and began sponsoring them one by one. In 1980, I went back to India and, with the aid of a wheelchair, brought my mother to the US to live with my family. When I tried to get some medical help for my new immigrant mother, there was nothing available. I was very disappointed, yet I refused to give up hope. We set out to care for her to the best of our ability.

On July 4, 1980, there was a new addition to our family. Sarah Ann was born and she brought more joy to the family. I was also glad that my mother would have a chance to see her and watch her grow. We recognized the nature of my mother in her so we named her after my mother. Her middle name came from Susie's mother. Now we had three children: an Indian, a Yankee, and the new Texan. Life was beautiful. We had gone from struggling to stable, from immigrants to citizens, and I'd gone from homeless to homeowner.

My mother truly enjoyed being with our family. In spite of her disability, she made a purposeful routine within our family life. I had a great sense of joy in seeing her with us in a better place. It was a blessing to have my mother see what I'd done in my life.

Unfortunately, within a year of her arrival, my mother passed away. She trusted in Jesus so we knew we'd see her again, which gave some comfort. I was still sad, not only at her passing, but by the limited help available to her in life. This experience only stirred in me an even greater desire to do something for needy people like my mother.

My mother had been a very God-fearing person. The week before she died, she was praying for others and the pastor of the church. She was gracious for allowing me to take care of her for her last days. Caring for my mother gave us a great deal of satisfaction and joy. It was an honor and privilege to serve her at the end of her life after all she'd suffered for my sake.

After being in the medical profession for many years, and taking care of hundreds of sick people, many of whom are needy and destitute, I had a heart to serve people. My heart went out to the needy and sick people like my mother. I was determined to do whatever I could to alleviate the pain and loneliness of their condition.

A search to help

It was during this time that the Lord helped me start a church in Ulsoor, Bangalore, along with a local pastor. I had learned of him when we sponsored his Bible school studies. When I went to see him, I spent one week with people who've lived in the slums. These people had almost no worldly possessions. They lived in huts with plastic tarps for roofs. They lived in very unsanitary conditions. We went on the streets and visited their homes to tell them of the good news of Jesus Christ. There were many who got saved and decided to be baptized in water during that week.

Many experienced true life changing joy by accepting Christ. Unfortunately, many of the women could not be baptized because they did not have a second pair of clothes to change in to. After that first visit to Bangalore, I made it a point to take white saris for all the women in the church so that everyone could partake in that experience. All of them became part of the full Gospel Church of Karnataka. The opportunity to be able to see the power and love of God bring hope in a person's life had a profound effect on me.

Midlife crisis

Another concern I had was that at my present job I had reached the top of what I could do with my training. In the corporate medical system there was not much I could not do on my own. I decided to go back to college and learn something new. Since I didn't have any clear direction at the beginning, I decided to begin with junior college.

I had also turned 40 and I was beginning to reflect on what had happened in my life to that point. Even though my life looked successful, I was not impressed with all that I had done. I thought about all my father had accomplished when he reached 40. I could not compare my accomplishments with his. In the next few days I continued to evaluate the situation and I began to assess different aspects of my life.

First, I evaluated my spiritual condition. The mighty hand of God worked in my life to bring me from a homeless runaway to an American citizen. But despite all the wonderful experiences I'd had with Jesus Christ, I was still not happy. I do not think I was living a victorious Christian life, even though I was very diligent about attending church.

Second, I looked at my professional life. I was in a reputed, well-liked profession and I could find more work than I could do. Yet I was neither happy, nor satisfied, with that either.

Third, I reflected upon my family life. I had a lovely wife and three smart children. Yet raising the family was a responsibility and even routine chores had become stressful.

Finally, I looked at my physical appearance. I had a gray beard, which made me look older than what I was. Even though I was not sick, I did not feel great. I had all the symptoms of a middle-aged man.

After this self-assessment of my past and present, I was not satisfied with all my accomplishments. I didn't, and don't, consider this depression, rather it was a spiritual intervention to fulfill the plan of God in my life. If God was going to use me as He had planned to use me, I needed to make changes in my life.

The first was a spiritual stagnation where everything had become routine. There was no victory or infilling of the Holy Spirit, especially during worship. I remembered in the early days of my new birth and the filling of the Holy Spirit, my prayers were spiritual warfare and I fought with God against demon possession and sickness. I had seen many people delivered.

It was at this time that there was a divine intervention in my life and my heart continued to ache for the things of God. One day while I was attending church, the Spirit of the Lord spoke to my heart that my physical appearance was not glorifying the Lord. Immediately upon hearing that from the Lord, I looked at myself in the mirror and I had to agree, so I shaved off my beard. For whatever reason the next day while I was worshiping at church, I experienced a change in me. After several years, I was really filled with the Holy Spirit and worshipped God in a new way. I left that service feeling much different than when I walked in. That week was different, I realized then that in the worship service I had had a spiritual renewal and it gave me an earnest desire to worship God in the Holy Spirit.

That realigned my priorities in life and for the first time I dedicated myself as a spiritual leader of my family. I made family prayer time a regular part of our lives. No one finished the day without spending time together praying and reading the Bible. This also became a time for us to talk to one another and discuss things in each other's lives. There were many nights when we sat for hours sharing with each other. It would be a source of great family strength in the days ahead when we faced problems. Even when I was not at home it was part of our family routine. God enabled us to experience the saying, "a family that prays together, stays together."

I also made changes in the way I gave to God. I had been a regular tither with my money since I had become a Christian. I gave to my church and to many missionary projects in India, but I saw a need to do more. I took *Luke 6:38*, where it says that we should give *"Give, and it will be given to you. A good measure, pressed down, shaken together and running over, will be poured into your lap."* and I made it a personal challenge. In the coming years I experienced the full awesome power of God in my financial situation.

I obeyed the word of God and became the spiritual leader of my family. I prayed for all of our family matters. When we faced a problem, I didn't try to fix it myself; I gave it over to God. As I did this, my relationship with my wife and children became much closer as well is filled with happiness and joy, and it gave me a new strength in my body. These decisions gave me a very young, energetic, and much more confident feeling. That renewed energy has continued on to the present day.

Going back to college

Going back to college after many years was a different experience for me. I was a little intimidated about going to a junior college with all the young people because I was not used to that in America. I spent a couple of years in the junior college system taking many basic courses like English, American History, Business, and Speech. I later found a program offered at the University of Houston-Clear Lake that was very attractive to me. I made an appointment with the Dean of the Healthcare Administration program. He explained to me how competitive jobs were and then he almost assured me I would not get a job as administrator in any institution. I could have felt discouraged and given up, but my desire would not let go. I told him that I was only looking for an education and not a job at that time. By January 1983, I joined the University of Houston-Clear Lake, where many large corporate business people, NASA employees, and other professional adults attended.

I felt much more comfortable there than and in the junior college, but the courses were very challenging. I had to work full time to raise our young family. Education was something I really wanted, but I could not give much time to my family and children because of it. Many times I could not see my children awake, play with them, or even see them going to school. I could not participate in many of their school activities either. Susie and the children were supportive and understanding. I was under a lot of stress, as I had to turn in papers, take exams, and study.

Many times they could not understand why I would get very irritated or upset over trivial matters. I was always tired because I was getting very little sleep and no time to relax. There was a never ending stream of term papers to write which involved large amounts of studying. Then I'd go to work where I was under a heavy burden of responsibilities. The little bit of time I did have at home I needed to simply experience peace and quiet.

Working three days a week, going to college full time, raising three children, and meeting all of our monthly needs left us with nothing much to save. It was a very challenging time just trying to make ends meet. I wanted to provide for our children with everything they wanted. They were growing up and I wanted them to go to nice schools, but we had just enough to make our bills with nothing left over. They were always told that Daddy only had $20 for shopping. I remember how Jacob wanted his favorite G.I. Joe toy, but we had to save for a while to be able to buy because it costs $6.25. By this time I was able to sponsor and bring my brothers and sisters, with their families, to America. We helped them get settled and establish themselves. Then I felt like God used me to replant my entire family from India to America. It reminded me of Genesis 4:5-8. In that verse Joseph is speaking with his brothers about his struggles and captivity.

While my brothers were loving and kind, I had lived many years in a captivity of rebellion, pain, sickness, and disease. However, all of those things led me to the American shore. I was given a new life, and new opportunity. The pain of rejection launched me ahead of my family and I was able to bring my brothers, parents, cousins, and family to a land of opportunity.

So while not sold as a slave by my brothers, I was still like a Joseph for my family. I was able to open the door for them, and then bring them along to experience the blessings I had.

Despite our financial struggles, during this time my spiritual life was improving. I started to learn more of the Christian life and a little more about a loving God who could also provide our needs. It put in me a desire to worship Him even more. From the time we moved to Houston, we had attended Lakewood Church. I remember the first time I attended a Sunday meeting in the old tin building we used to meet in. There was a missionary who had come from South America who needed some kind of vehicle. Pastor John Osteen took a collection and within a few minutes gladly gave this missionary more than he needed. I felt so happy with the pastor of the church because they were willing to give to the work of the Lord in other places.

In 1983, we joined a small local Malayalee fellowship, a Dallas-based Indian church which had a branch in Houston. Even though it was a small fellowship, we liked the idea of an intimate spiritual encounter and a personal involvement to shoulder work of the Lord in Houston among the Keralite community. While attending, we as a family experienced many spiritual blessings. Even though I had very little experience in the Malayalee Pentecostal fellowships, I really enjoyed the worship and the spiritual aspects of life and the church.

In the beginning of the church, our branch in Houston was an off shoot of a Dallas fellowship. Therefore, the pastor had to come from Dallas to conduct meetings then jumped on a plane back to Dallas. In His time, God really prompted us to get involved with that church in spite of all the other responsibilities we had. I can honestly say that I never missed a church service. I had the opportunity to dedicate much of my time to the church and, even though our income was not much, we tithed regularly in addition to giving offerings. Giving became a spontaneous action. The word says, "It is better to give than to receive." We not only believed that, but it became a reality in our lives.

Healing of asthma

From 1983-1984, I suffered severely from breathing difficulties, which I never suffered from before. It got so bad that I went to my doctor for a checkup. After examining me, and conducting several tests, he said I had bronchial asthma. This particular asthma requires the use of medicine over an indefinite period of time. He wrote a prescription for me and I went to get it filled. While I was on my way to the pharmacy the Lord reminded me of my mother. She had suffered from asthma for 40 years and, in the end, her treatments had led to hypertension, stroke, and paralysis, all without providing her much relief.

I remembered all of this around the second anniversary of her death. I'd had symptoms for about a year at this point. I realize that the devil was planning the same thing for me. I set the prescription aside and decided I would not be taking the medicine.

Over the next few days the asthma became worse. It was nearly impossible to breathe whether I was sitting or standing. One early morning, at about 5 a.m., I jumped out of bed, gasping for breath. I thought I was going to die. I had the strong urge to call 911, but I decided not to. I sat in my recliner and began to praise God. After a while I fell asleep in the chair. When I woke up a few hours later I felt completely normal. Asthma left me that day and has never returned again. That day I received the true understanding of James 4:7, "Submit yourselves, then, to God. Resist the devil, and he will flee from you." I realize the devil was a defeated foe and we as Christians have the power to stand against his attacks.

Finally, on May 5, 1985 we stood in the hot sun for several hours for my graduation ceremony. I graduated from college with a 3.0 grade point average. In the presence of my wife and three children at the age of 42, I received my Bachelors of Science degree in health service administration. It was one of my life's happiest moments. I said goodbye to some very nice people who had become friends and graduated along with me.

One of them was Debra Sweeney from Missouri. She was very helpful to me during those three years of study at the University of Houston. Many times she read from the text as I listen and tried to study in the library. That was how I was able to make many of my tests.

I really wanted to celebrate that day with my family but I did not have enough money for a good lunch. But we were satisfied with what little we had. Now the challenge before me was to get an appropriate job for my education. I was nearly burned out with nursing. I had excelled in the profession for 15 years, but I needed a new direction.

When I graduated from the University of Houston-ClearLake, the economy had radically changed. The world oil glut caused many oil refineries and related industries to shut down or lay off most of their staff. There was a new influx of people moving into Houston in the late 70s and early 80s who had lost their jobs along with their savings, houses, and cars. Houston was undergoing a recession in the mid-80s when I graduated from college and looking for a job became extremely difficult.

As a new graduate, a middle-aged man, foreign-born, and with an accent, it was not easy to be accepted into the job market, especially in the higher-level administrative jobs. Yet that did not stop me from trying to find a job. I even traveled to other cities outside of Houston.

While I continued working full-time at Eastway General Hospital in Houston, God led me to Grand Prairie, Texas where I spoke with a hospital director about a job opportunity with them. She offered me a management position in nursing, which I declined. Later, she called back saying there was an administrative coordinator position on the weekends that was a full-time position. It was a large hospital with many new programs, 24 hour surgery, and educational research. My new position required me to work from Friday afternoon until Monday morning in Grand Prairie, a 285 mile commute each way.

The job included all facilities, a nice office with a handful of keys to other facilities. I had to manage the facility with very little outside help. I found it very challenging. There was an average of 100 to 150 local staff during any given shift. I had to commute between Houston and Grand Prairie, which meant leaving Houston on Friday morning and returning Monday evening. I did this for one and a half years. Again I enrolled in college to finish my MBA. The commute to Grand Prairie was getting harder every time I'd had to do it, even though I enjoyed the work. I had built up a good rapport with the administration and they were willing to help me.

Later I resigned from the job at Grand Prairie and began to work with the Texas Medical Foundation in Houston. Even though the salary was less, it gave me a lot of needed experience that would help me accomplish what I wanted to do in later days. Also, I could be home every night.

All of these things help me to understand how the corporate world functioned and I started to work on something of my own. During this time I had undergone training and received a license in real estate sales, insurance sales, and was a notary public, but my heart was not content in any of these things.

One day in 1986 I thought about leaving Houston and moving to Dallas, or some other city, in order to find a better paying job. The job I had did not earn enough to meet our needs, so I began to pray with the prophet in our church. The Spirit of the Lord spoke to me through the Prophet saying, "I have planted you in Houston and I will establish you there." I was also assured that I was going to be blessed and be able to build a new house for my family to live in. The spirit of the Lord even revealed the description of the house. In human eyes, it was impossible. I was just barely making it with my present job and I had no savings. I could not see finding a well paying job in Houston, but I remembered the story of the Prophet Elijah when he was waiting for rain in Israel.

I Kings 18: 41-45 "Elijah said to King Ahab, "Get thee up, eat and drink: for there is the sound of a heavy rain ....Meanwhile, the sky grew black with clouds, the wind rose, and the heavy rain came on.........." I fully believed that God can open doors for me.

Starting my first company

In the early part of 1987, I was frustrated with all the corporate jobs that brought me no satisfaction. So I decided not to seek a new job. I resigned all the jobs I had and sat at home. For almost 2 1/2 weeks I refuse to go to apply for any other jobs.

During this period, I had plans to start a home health care business to reach and serve the needy people, especially elderly in their homes. Even though I had done this kind of work in India, I had never done it in America. Working for somebody and getting a regular paycheck had always been easier than running an organization with increasing responsibility.

I considered purchasing a franchise from a larger organization so that I could learn from them, but there were so many regulatory checks and administrative duties with those. Also, I had no financial back up to start a business. However, I refused to sit around defeated. I sought the Lord for direction and one day, out of the blue, I got in the car and drove to Grand Prairie. I went to the same place I worked in Grand Prairie to meet with one of the vice presidents of the hospital. Usually, to see such a person one had to make an appointment weeks in advance. While working in Grand Prairie I learned a great deal about health care administration. I also became friends with many of my superiors. One of them was Judy, the Vice President of the hospital.

When I drove in that day, she was standing in the parking lot talking to someone. As soon as she saw me, she walked towards me, greeted me and asked where I was going. When I told her I had come to meet with her she said that we could talk while we got some coffee. I talked to her about my desire to start a freestanding home healthcare service. Without any hesitation, she called one of her directors who was the head of the home health Department and instructed them to provide me with all the necessary guidance to get started. She was happy to help but warned me that it was a long, drawn out process to get a license in Texas at that time. Despite that, she even made the appointment for the pre-survey conference with the Texas department of Health.

Within the next few months I was able to set up the foundation of the home healthcare service. There were many more things they had to do, not the least of which was securing the state license to operate. However, I did not have the money to pay the initial fee.

At this point it had been several weeks since I had a job. The needs were increasing but I did not want to look for a nursing job. I wasn't sure what to do. I was sitting at home; everyone else had gone to school and work. I received a phone call from a lady who had gone to college with me. Connie needed a relief weekend supervisor. She wanted to hire me for her organization.

The job was perfect for me at that time because I was getting the policy and procedures ready for the state survey to obtain the license to run a home health care company. There were so many regulatory details, forms to create, and procedural details which I had to do by trial and error. I also had to set up an office and a certain number of employees to perform each specific task.

She offered me $1000 bonus if I took the job- the exact amount I need to apply for state license. I took the job, got my bonus of $1000, and applied for the license. In a few weeks I had to get everything ready for the Texas Department of Health. By the grace of God, I was licensed in the State of Texas to run a freestanding home health agency.

In December of 1987 God enabled me to start "Tender Loving Care Health Services of Texas." I may even be the first Indian immigrant to have a business entity of that nature in the United States. The beginning years of the company were very challenging. I found myself having to wear many hats in my company. I was the chief executive officer, financial officer, director, manager, worker, marketing person etc. In the beginning there was plenty of work, but no money coming in. After nine months of working I earned my first check, $640. I continued to work at the old job on the weekends. Monday through Friday, I worked in my business.

It did not take much time to make that company a two or three million-dollar revenue-producing company. Life was very stressful as I was starting to live in the corporate world. There was money, power, responsibility, and liability. And yet none of these things made me forget God, or my dependency on him. I can clearly see that only with God's help could I do all these things without falling.

In 1989, a couple of years after the first business had started, my family built our new home. It was a fulfillment of prophecy. God sees things before we see them. In 1986 when there was nothing to see, no money, not even a steady job, and I wanted to leave Houston, God's promise came to me, and after a while, he began establishing me there.

I remember when Pastor John Osteen preached about building a new church in 1986. When everything was unfavorable, God told him to "build". I used to rejoice and to shed tears of joy for how the Lord works in his people's lives. No matter who you are, if God promises something, he will deliver. In 1986, when the Spirit of the Lord spoke through the prophet of God, I did not question or doubt God. I also did not have enough faith to see beyond the present situation, so I did not put much hope in accomplishing anything. I just continued to do what I had to do in my day to day life and continue to trust God for all of our needs.

On July 3, 1990, we moved to our new home. It was a nice home. We each picked things we wanted in our rooms. Everyone selected their favorite color of paint, carpet, and cabinets. We were very happy. God enabled us to be debt free on the house within one year of building it.

On July 4 we celebrated Sarah's 10th birthday in her new house. We were happy, and somewhat proud, of what we had accomplished. We were very thankful to God for fulfilling his promise when we had nothing.

But in 1991, 3 days before Christmas, it was ruined by a fire. It had only been a year and a half since we moved in and we displaced for almost 9 months after the fire. But even then I didn't ask God why this was happening to me. I strongly believed that if he could do all the things he had done so far, he could do things even better. Again God spoke to us through this experience and taught us not to trust in anything we have in this world, because everything is temporary and perishable, but only to depend on him for all of our needs. Strong faith in God brought a very strong foundation in our lives.*1 John 2:17 "The world and its desires pass away, but the man who does the will of God lives forever."* After many months of negotiations, our house was rebuilt much better than its original condition. We added many more things to the house to make it even more comfortable for us as a home.

The home health business was growing well. There was better cash flow, and more employees. We were looking for more opportunities to increase our services on different levels. Home infusion was a flourishing business at that time. At the end of 1990, God enabled me to start another corporation in partnership with another person called IVPB Infucare, Inc., a home infusion pharmacy. In the end, when the partners could not make a lot of quick money they left, and I ended up having a large liability on my hands. However, God finally changed that situation and in two years it became a profitable entity. The home health industry was rapidly growing all over the country. In 1991, after several government audits, Tender Loving Care Home Health Services registered as a corporation, called Mathai Incorporated.

In 1993, we established a company called EJS medical, named after my children. EJS medical had a complete line of medical supplies and was a durable medical equipment company. Even though there were increased responsibilities, and much more income, I felt that only with faith in God and a total dependency on him could I lead and manage all these businesses. Whatever future decisions I had to make, I only made them after waiting upon the Lord.

Among the people who became involved with us over the years, only a few rejoiced in our progress. Many became jealous in their heart towards us. This included people from our families, coworkers, and fellow believers. It was very disheartening to not have the support of these people, but there was no chance we'd forget God or stop trusting Him.

My life was now blessed and increasingly everyone wanted a piece. All kinds of government services, big and small, noticed our growth. By this time, the business is had grown to have an annual payroll of $2 to $2.5 million. In spite of the increased income, our lifestyle remained almost the same. We were much more involved in the church life, family prayer, and trusting God for almost everything. When God entrusted us with wealth and placed more responsibilities in our hands, I felt a sense of responsibility towards him.

We continued to be fully involved in our local Mayalee church, shouldering the responsibility of a higher level both physically and financially. Many changes began happening to the organization. Many branches started in different cities and membership increased in different areas. Many also began trying to get leadership positions. In a very peculiar way the church started to go forward. Church buildings started to be erected in different places. The fundamental principle started to change. The headquarters, without the proper guidance or supervision, appointed several pastors for the church branches, many of them being political appointees of the organization.

Because of the Church philosophy of nonparticipation with others, the local members were increasingly isolated. They are more secluded from many other churches and their philosophy for others made it sound a lot like a cult. It wasn't that, but rather a very strict, old fashioned, Pentecostal church.

Certain times it sounded very nice but increasingly people began to leave. Since they discouraged participation outside of the Malayalam church, I was not able to participate in some of the ministries I wanted to be involved in.

Despite this, I was able to start the church in Bangalore. We continued to worship with this group until the oppressive spirit stole all the joy of worship from me and we left. Instead of feeling a sense of spiritual freedom, I felt that there was a spiritual oppression and bondage taking place. I felt the anointing God gave me for a ministry with no opportunity because of the lack of spiritual movement.

By this time the church we had started in Bangalore in the 1980 had grown enough to have a worship facility. But in the 1980s when I was struggling with many other things, I could not imagine ever raising enough funds to build a church there. I had a strong desire to build a church for the people of the Ulsoor slum in Bangalore. I had approached one of the prominent mission organizations to help save some money to build a church there, but the person I had contacted never replied. I wrote to the believers in Bangalore of the situation and they replied saying, "We understand. When the Lord strengthens your hand, you buy the building for the church." That broke my heart, but encouraged me to trust God to provide this for the people. In the early 1990s with God's strength, I was able to buy a small building for the church in the middle of the Bangalore city. On my next trip in 1993, we inaugurated the "Full Gospel Church of Karnataka" in its own building. Our pastor and fellow members from our home church in the United States, along with my family, join the congregation in Bangalore for this momentous occasion. To this day I continue to support the work in Bangalore.

Chapter 9

Call of God to the Ministry

I was at the peak of my life in every aspect in 1993. By this time, I had three profitable businesses in four officers in different parts of Texas that were experiencing 200 to 300% growth annually. Moreover, we were looking in various places to aggressively expand our business. We had a great deal of material wealth, a good house, nice cars, and very good health. The entire family was doing well.

We were enjoying life after so many years of struggle. Yet I could feel a void somewhere in my life which was not fulfilled-my service to God. In spite of all the success that we were enjoying, something was missing. This was when the Spirit of the Lord started to deal with me. The burning desire to do more for His kingdom still filled me. Participating in the local church was not enough. I needed more.

One Sunday afternoon all resting after the church service I heard a voice saying,

"Go back to your people."

The thought startled me and I sat up suddenly and walked out of the bedroom to the patio in the backyard. I found a chair to sit in and called my younger daughter over to me.

"The Lord just told me to go back to my people."

She replied, "We are your people and we are all here."

By that time, not only was my immediate family with me, but God had enabled me to bring my parents, three brothers, two sisters, and their families to The States. I had no immediate relatives in India, except some distant cousins. There was no personal interest for me to go to India. I had given my inherited property to my father to do with whatever he wanted. I had, so far, not acquired anything in India. No one expected me to visit them or do anything since I had been gone from my hometown since 1961. By this time it had been 8 1/2 years since I had even visited India.

But I'd heard the voice of God. And he was sending me.

After hearing the voice of God, I searched my heart. Many thoughts went through my mind. I had no specific group I could call *my people*. The last group of people with whom I had had contact in India was a group of outcasts I'd worked with: leprosy patients. They lived in different parts of South India, on the streets, in asylums or Leprosy Hospitals and spoke different languages.

The other group of people was the people of my hometown. Many of the adults I had known 32 years ago had now passed away. The younger people might not even know me. Whenever I visited my hometown I had to introduce myself as *the son of* or *the brother of* someone, because no one knew me personally. This always limited my ability to reestablish a relationship anyplace.

However, in obedience to the call of God, my family decided to visit India in 1993. After many years of being gone, we traveled extensively to reacquaint ourselves with the country. I visited as many churches as possible during that visit. We also went to Bangalore and inaugurated a new church building we purchased for the full Gospel Church of Karnataka that had been established in 1980.

Again in 1994 I went to India, this time with another pastor, intending to do mission work. We went to different cities in India and spoke at many meetings. We came to Pandalam, my hometown, and conducted a two-day Crusade. We were happy with the good response we received. Many people were saved and sent to different churches. We also visited the Gulf countries of Dubai, Abu Dhabi, and Bahrain. At that time an outreach team was started in Pandalam. We went around to different places to conduct open air meetings, crusades, and house to house visits. It lasted for several months in spite of great opposition from the Hindu Fanatics (R.S.S.) and other people. The R.S.S. beat some of our workers and ultimately their work was limited to certain areas.

Then again in 1995, I visited different churches in Bombay, Bangalore, Dharwar, New Delhi, Nilambur and Pandalam. Everywhere I went, I was able to share my story with people. My testimony touched many people and we saw many come to Christ.

When I took these trips I brought as many clothes and as much money as I could from home to share with the needy. Many times these gifts gave me an opportunity to share the Gospel. And on these trips I was able to build houses for individual families and repair many other houses. We bought cows and rickshaws for the poor to help them provide for themselves. The help went through the local pastors to the needy people.

God's provision in every need

My daughter, Elizabeth, graduated from college in December of 1995. She was 23 years. We suggested that it might be a good time for her to marry and she agreed with us. She was always a very obedient daughter and always wanted to please God and her parents in whatever she did. When we suggested she get married she said that she wanted to follow our traditional manner and have an arranged marriage. She had been living in America since she was one year old and she had studied all her life in America. However, when it came to finding a life partner, she wholeheartedly agreed to have the parents select her groom, just like her parents had had. She was strong in her faith and confident that the Lord would bring the one He had chosen in to her life.

So, as I prepared to leave for India on a mission trip in January of 1996, I prayed to God, "I'm going to India to do your work, and I would like to find a suitable man for my daughter. However, I do not want to spend any time looking for him or going from place to place to see different proposals (prospects)." I wanted God's complete and perfect will in this matter.

The mission trip was for a heavily scheduled three weeks. I had meetings and programs in many places and we were able to bless many people. During this visit, I received one proposal from a family, but did not take any time to go inquire about it. My last Sunday in Trivandrum, after a full day of activities in church, I decided to stop by the family's home on my way to the airport. I showed the local pastor the address of the proposed young man and we went to their home. When I arrived the young man was not home but I was able to meet with his parents. We spoke for about 20 minutes and they gave me his picture. Then I had to rush to the airport to catch my plane.

As I prepared to leave their home the Spirit of God spoke to my heart: "You saw only one girl and you married her. In the same way you do not have to look elsewhere for your daughter." I took this as a confirmation from God that He had chosen this man for my daughter.

On my return trip, I attempted to meet my old friend Armugam in Pondichery, but I did not have his address or phone number. Miraculously his son Murali came to Madras and met me. He informed me that his father was sick with kidney failure and he could not come. I shared Jesus with Murali and he accepted Him into his life in the airport lounge. He left with the joy of salvation. I continued to have contact with Mr. Armugam and he gave me the opportunity to help him with some of his medical care expenses for treatments and dialysis. It was a real blessing to be able to help him once again.

A Chance meeting

One day, while having lunch at Luby's cafeteria, I had a chance meeting with Sister Dodie Osteen. During the conversation she told me that she was going to ask Pastor John Osteen to send me an invitation to attend the upcoming pastor's and leader's conference, hosted by Pastor Osteen and the Lakewood Church. I received my invitation the next day. This happened three days before my daughter, Elizabeth, Susie and I were leaving for India to meet the young man about the proposed marriage.

We weren't sure what to expect so we informed the pastors from our home church that we were about to leave the country. The night before our departure there was an emergency committee meeting at the Malayalee church we had attended for many years. The meeting was not conducted in a spiritual atmosphere. We listened for hours, heartbroken at what we were witnessing. Then, with tears in our eyes, my son Jacob and I decided to leave that meeting. Until then, I had only heard about church politics, but that day I saw it all, and I will never forget it. With a heavy heart, I left for India the next day.

God's provision was with us. We felt God's presence with us during the whole trip, and He met all our needs. My daughter met the proposed young man, his name is Roy, and his family members. They liked each other and agreed to have the official engagement ceremony at the end of the same week. We had a grand engagement party in Trivandrum. There were almost 400 guests and family members from both sides. After the celebration in India, we came back to Houston on June 6.

The pastors and leaders conference at Lakewood Church that Mrs. Osteen had invited me to was from June 10-14. That meant I was able to attend the entire conference after my trip. The conference was presented as a challenge to those in attendance. We were reminded of our responsibility as the body of Christ to reach lost souls. Pastor John Osteen shared a powerful message that reminded us that every day people died without Jesus. His concern for humanity encouraged, touched and awakened my heart. A new burning desire to do something for God grew in me. It was at that conference that God helped me to get a sense of direction to establish an independent ministry to serve God.

The praise and worship during the conference and the freedom of the Holy Spirit freed my heart from the bondage of religious and church issues that had been weighing me down. The simple teaching of the Word of God penetrated our hearts. The word of God, and the joy of witnessing, gave me a renewed spiritual revival in my life. After many years in a church where there was no revival, it was a joy to see the simple gospel of Jesus Christ change lives. There was not one time I came home from church without shedding tears and rejoicing in the Lord.

Elizabeth and Roy planned to get married in Houston during the month of September of 1996. We had only a few months to prepare for the many formalities before the wedding. Elizabeth's fiancé had to get a fiancé visa and his parents also had to get visiting visas. We needed to find an appropriate place to conduct the wedding. Even though we had lived in America for more than 20 years, there were many formalities to meet if we chose to follow the traditional ways. All the preparations were well on the way. We had everything in place and hired a wedding consultant to coordinate and arrange everything exactly the way my daughter and her fiancé wanted. They had chosen the grand ballroom at the Four Seasons Hotel in downtown Houston. The guests consisted of the families from both sides, friends, church members, well-known Indian pastors from Houston and from other cities, business associates, and our employees at Mathai Inc. and their families.

Everything was progressing well, but behind all this planning, we were preoccupied by a growing problem. Since she was having an arranged marriage my daughter wanted to respect the customs of our culture as much as possible. Unfortunately, the Malayalee church was seeking to exercise much more control over the ceremonial aspects of the wedding than we felt necessary. As a loving father to my daughter, I was willing to compromise and do anything to make our daughter happy. These requests, however, were running counter to the desires of my daughter and her future husband.

A week before the wedding, despite long days and nights of negotiations, the church continued with their demands. All other wedding arrangements were progressing nicely. Roy and his parents obtained visas to come to the USA and arrived two weeks before the wedding. We were able to invite our relatives from all over America. Negotiations continued on to the last week without an agreement being reached with the church.

God heard the prayer of a needy man again and arranged for all the appropriate people outside this church to help us conduct the wedding. The overseer of the Church of God from my home church in Kerala and the Overseer of the

Church of God from Texas agreed to solemnize the wedding without any hesitation.

All of the arrangements were finalized just a few days before the wedding. A compromised agreement was reached with the church and they agreed to conduct a wedding. By the grace of God, Elizabeth and Roy were married in the presence of 400 invited guests, relatives, families, business associates, employees, friends, church members, and 16 pastors.

We give glory and honor to the Almighty God. After going through months of pain and hurt we decided there was no reason to go through the same experience of slavery to religion and its practices. God called us to worship and serve him and rejoice in the freedom and liberty in Christ Jesus.

Galatians 5:1 "it is for freedom that Christ has set us free, stand firm then and do not let yourself be burdened again by the yoke of slavery."

There was no more joy attending a fellowship with the same people, therefore we left the Malayalee church to find a new group of Christians. Our children spent a good part of their childhood in that church. They did not know any other church routines and customs. So it was going to require learning for all of us.

A new church home

With all the circumstances that took place during this time, we made some decisions about what we as a family needed for our spiritual life. We felt bruised after what we had gone through. It was a time for us as a family to heal and look to the future, so we made the decision to attend Lakewood Church regularly.

Lakewood was a large church with about 8,000 people on an average Sunday morning. Pastor Osteen preached for almost all the meetings. He had so much to give to people spiritually and always thrived being able to do more things. He had opened our hearts to love all people, rejoice in others' joy, and be burdened by others' sorrow.

The church we had participated in before was small so many of the members took lots of responsibility for everyday operation of the church. We made a decision as a family that we would strictly be involved with worship and fellowship only.

We realized a new spiritual freedom in worship. No longer did we have someone else to intercede to God. God dealt with our hearts through the Word of God to cleanse, heal, and deliver us. It was very difficult in the beginning for our family to adjust. We had also been taught that it was only through the church pastor or the prophets that people could be healed through the laying on of hands. Now, we started to feel much more freedom and responsibility for our own spiritual lives than when we had depended on others. Though our peace was disrupted, God had been so kind and faithful in the times of our troubles and needs.

He started to deal with us individually in our own spiritual matters. Elizabeth and Roy chose to attend an Indian church. My biggest concern for Sarah was the fact that she'd never been to any other church. But during this time she found a renewed passion in her Christian walk and began to experience a new depth in her relationship with Christ. It began in her high school Bible study where new heights of worship and learning the Word of God took place. The adjustment might have been difficult for her. But now Susie, Jacob, Sarah and I continue to attend Lakewood Church.

The burden for lost souls was very real in Pastor John Osteen's transforming sermons. It has brought hundreds of people from all walks of life to a saving knowledge of Christ.

They were healed from all kinds of sicknesses, habits, and problems in life. The spiritual deliverance that Jesus Christ brings is not just for a selected group. It is sad to see people cling to their own customs instead of accepting the free gift of God. The desire to share the Gospel with others grew daily in my life. Each believer is responsible to do the will of God and minister to bring the lost souls to saving knowledge of God. We are happier now and continue to be members of this church.

Going with the purpose

In 1997, I went back to India. Again I traveled to many cities and villages with the Gospel of Jesus Christ and preached in many churches and with their ministries. Still I didn't feel that I was fulfilling God's call to go back to my people, so I asked God to direct me in the right path. Finally, I went back to my hometown of Pandalam and I prayed several days in the hotel room I was staying in. I prayed for the deliverance of the people of my hometown. God gave me a burden for that place and on that trip many people came with many needs and prayers. Many got saved and healed and I was able to help many people out financially and materially. I was starting to be known there and I was directed in many ways to serve the people there. I worked among people of all faiths, denominations, and religions.

I initiated outreach teams with some of the pastors and evangelists who showed an interest to work in that area. Since my trips were short, and I do not have time to properly direct or manage the people, I looked for a reliable person to continue to work there. Unfortunately, after only a few months few pastors remained who could continue to do outreach work. I made a second trip at the end of 1997 and visited many places, but focused on starting a lasting work and Pandalam. In each of my trips God did many unusual things. God miraculously healed and delivered many people. I never thought that I had any kind of ability to do God's work, but He was teaching and preparing me for His ministry. I had witnessed to people of other national origins and the salvation message was well accepted.

While traveling on my second mission trip in 1997, I planned to go to New Delhi to work with a pastor. While passing through Bangkok, the Spirit of the Lord spoke to my heart to go to Colombo, Sri Lanka, instead of New Delhi. I changed my flight plans and arrived in Colombo at midnight. I'd never been to Colombo before and I had no one to see there. When I arrived, I had to wait until 4:30 a.m. for my connecting flight to Madras. Everyone else left the transit lounge except one passenger who had traveled with me on the same flight from Bangkok. His name was Abood, he was a native Muslim of the Maldives islands. He told me that almost 100% of the population in Maldives was Muslim. This created the opportunity to share the Gospel with him and he accepted Jesus Christ as His personal savior. We prayed together until half an hour before his flight left.

When I had left Bangkok I really did not know why God had asked me to go to Colombo, but after Abood accepted Jesus as his personal savior and left with Christian literature to go back to Maldives, I understood God's plan. That nation is now touched with the Gospel of Jesus Christ.

I continued my journey to Madras where I met Murali, my friend Arumugam's son. If you remember, Mr. Arumugam was dying but had gotten saved and healed in 1972 and lived another 25 years. I was informed that he passed away on February 19, 1997 after living a full life. Our merciful God allowed him to see his children grow up, marry and have children of their own. When I heard of his death, I was deeply saddened and had cried in my office. I had then decided that I should visit his widow and children on my next visit. So, from Madras, Murali and I got on a bus and arrived at Pondichery that evening. There Mrs. Armugam and her daughter Vijay accepted Jesus Christ into their lives as Murali had on one of my previous visits in the Madras Airport.

More changes and adjustments

1997 was a year of many events in our life. After 10 years in business, and after having my daughter's wedding and attending a new church, we realized that we did not have many solid friends to depend upon: not even relatives. All the acquaintances we'd had for the past 13 years were mostly through the Malayalee church. Above all, our youngest daughter Sarah graduated from high school and was going out of town for college.

We felt alone and isolated. Yet we did not give up. We had seen God do so much in and through us, so we trusted him. On one side, we were facing a lot of isolation but on the other side God was preparing us as a family to be strong in Him and continue to keep the faith. When external things diminished, God strengthened us internally. We had so many things to be thankful to God for. First of all, He had separated us from the bondage of religious and spiritual dependency on people. God continue to add blessings to our life. On September 4, 1997, Liz and Roy had a son, a very cute boy named Christopher. That changed many of our priorities in life. It also brought back a wonderful sense of ease into our family. We had finally become grown ups, and grandparents. Christopher gave back the unpredictable nature to our family.

On December 8, 1997 we celebrated the 10th anniversary of our company Tender Loving Care Health Services and we're able to do it in a grand way. We had a banquet at the Wyndham Warwick Hotel with about 150 invited guests, current staff members, and some from the past, business associates, and doctors. All of our employees were given service and merit awards. But even while we were celebrating, I knew there was something happening with our industry.

The government had changed a lot of regulations and many constraints were coming. The cash flow started to diminish. In the early part of 1998, I had to lay off a large number of employees and downsize my business. A lot of liability started accumulating and we could not satisfy many of the employees and other business associates. We started to hear every day about government auditing. There were many things to be concerned and worried about. Daily the need for money increased and the income started to decrease. By the end of 1998, we almost had to close down the business.

In 1994, I had learned of another concept of medical care. It was neither a new concept nor was it very common. It was care associated with the end stages of living, or hospice care. In the early part of 1995 I went to England to learn and research more about palliative care. I was impressed with this concept of care. In May 1995, I was licensed to start a hospice care company. I started East Harris County Hospice Services Inc. It was incorporated in the state of Texas. The home hospice was in Houston with a multidisciplinary team of staff to care for the terminally ill patients. This team included doctors, nurses, social workers, chaplains, bereavement counselors, and volunteers to address different aspects of human needs. Besides medical care we sought to help them mentally, and spiritually

At that time I did not realize the regulatory or financial impact of this company. I was just concentrating on, and fascinated with, the humanistic approach, especially addressing the spiritual needs of the patients and their families. During all the years of my medical work and experience, I had been limited in addressing and helping people with the spiritual aspects of their life. I never missed the opportunity to encourage someone with the eternal love of God and the message of salvation. In hospice, spiritual care was one of the aspects of palliative care, so we were able to offer to pray for someone in need of prayer and share with them the Gospel. Many patients and families came to know the love of God through our program.

We encouraged our chaplains to take an evangelical approach rather than an ecumenical approach in spiritual care. This hospice program was very dear to me regardless of the cost. The company progressed fairly well but was never able to capture a bigger market because of our larger involvement with home health care.

In 1997, we started a community-based Laundromat in a low income part of Houston. There we had regular Christian outreach programs through Gospel distribution and counseling the youth. None of these businesses were really giving the desired financial gain to continue, but God's protecting hand was with us throughout it all to keep us from falling. We continued to experience reductions in income and health problems where God directly intervened, but we remembered the Word of God says it best in *2 Corinthians 12:9, "My grace is sufficient for thee, for my strength is made perfect in weakness."*

At the same time the unending desire to serve God kept growing in my heart. I thought many of these changes in my business were ways that God was preparing me to take my final concentration off my business and place more time and energy into the ministry I was involved in.

Chapter 10

Beginning of Mathai Outreach Ministries

Even though I was involved in many spiritual activities at church, I still had a void and an unsatisfied feeling. On many of the mission trips I took to India, and other neighboring, countries I was reminded of the story of David and Goliath. The enemy is a giant and he is well protected in favorable surroundings. The roaring of the enemy was real and terrifying. The stronghold of the enemy was powerful.

In most of the places I know in India, every street has a temple and every temple has a god. In other neighboring Asian countries, many of the gods or idols are imported from India. Over one billion people in India worship millions of gods. I don't know the names or characters of them. Maybe my scholarly father could have explained a lot of them, but one thing I have noticed is that these gods lacked the basic character of the true God. *Galatians 4:8 we read, "Formerly, when you did not know God, you were slaves to those who by nature are not gods."*

Most of these gods are the cause of sin, sickness, demon possession, bondage, poverty, and unbelief. Many religions are built around these gods and given different names. They worship them out of fear of retaliation from offended gods. As long as you ponder and worship these evil spirits, they will follow and keep you in bondage without any deliverance. As long as you worship these spirits, you will also be bound in slavery.

Christianity in India is almost 2000 years old. As you know, the apostle Thomas, one of the 12 disciples of Jesus Christ known as "doubting Thomas" came to India and established Christianity there in the first century. He was a martyr in India, but because many giants like Goliath were in the land, the Gospel has never grown as it should, considering its age. It is very sad to see that my homeland is less than 3% professing Christians, even after 2000 years.

There have been many missionary movements, crusades, and other Christian activities that have taken place in India. Most of the Christians found in India are located in Kerala, the southernmost part of India. God has raised up thousands of men and women from Kerala to stand for God and take the Gospel to other parts of India and the world.

On many of my early trips to India I felt that I was going back and forth with help to the poor or needy and to help some churches and local pastors financially. Like the little David carrying food for his brothers in the Saul's army. On one of my mission trips it was as if I was going back and forth like little David. David wasn't strong enough to go in to battle, but he was big enough to obey and bless his brothers. He brought them food. However, once he'd delivered the food, the real power came in the spirit he brought. He delivered his people through the power of God.

I realized that the physical or material needs of the poor are not the only enemy in the land. There was a real enemy who, like Goliath, holds the people captive and in fear. In India it is the power of darkness and demonic spirit which causes all the poverty and sickness.

Ever since I heard the voice of God telling me to go back to my people in 1993, in obedience to that call, I have been visiting some of these enemy's strong hold areas in different parts of India, and other countries. During this time in India many anti-Christian and anti-missionary movements have sprung up all over. The Australian missionary, Mr. Graham Stains, and his two innocent children were set on fire in their van and killed in one area. Christian workers have been beaten and tortured in many different parts of India, churches and houses have been burned. Our own missionaries have been stopped and beaten many times and their lives have been threatened without them receiving any protection or support from the government or the local police.

Yet we never considered that these were the giants. We called them external and physical threats, but in many places, the poverty, sickness, and bondage to the demonic spirits were manifested in different ways. The sacrificial death of Jesus Christ, on the cross and the shedding of His blood, brought the salvation and freedom from the bondage and slavery of serving the gods who did not have the nature of the Almighty God.

When David realized that taking the roasted grain and the loaves of bread for his brothers in King Saul's Army was not enough to defeat Goliath and win the victory over the Philistines, he had to defeat the enemy in battle by collecting a few smooth stones, put them in the sling and start striking the Philistine on his forehead.

Present-day India needs Spirit filled God's people to fight the enemy rather than taking the material help for the poor. Giving money and other materials to the missionaries in India are essential, but won't be enough in the present condition. We must personally go to India and confront the enemy face to face.

Our battle is a spiritual battle and it requires spiritual strength. When I look back over my life I could say few things like little David said to King Saul in *1 Samuel 17:34-35, "Your servant has been keeping his father's sheep. When a lion or bear came in and carried off a sheep from the flock, I went after it, struck it, and rescued the sheep from its mouth. When it turned on me, I seized it by its hair, struck it, and killed it. The Lord who delivered me from the paws of the lion and the bear will deliver me from the hand of the Philistines."*

When I looked back at my own life the mighty hand of God had delivered me: a dropout, low self-esteem, rebellious runaway who lived on the streets as a homeless and hopeless person. I'd been in bondage to bad habits, in the claws of demonic spirits, and had sickness with a blind eye. Yet he saved me, set me free, he helped me and delivered me from many bondages. He gave me sight in my eye, took my shame, low self-esteem, and poverty and gave me the opportunity to find a noble profession and established me beyond anyone's expectations.

He gave me everything in life. As in *Psalms 40:2-3, "He lifted me out of the slimy pit, out of the mud and mire; he set my feet on a rock and gave me a firm place to stand. He put a new song in my mouth, a hymn of praise to our God. Many will see and hear and put their trust in the Lord."*

When I looked at Maslow's Need Hierarchy Theory with my life, I saw that I had climbed many steps to reach a self-actualization and arrive at the full potential of my life with so very little.

When I look at all of these accomplishments, I know that it was not done by my merit or qualifications. The Word of God says in *Zachariah 4:6, "Not by might nor by power, but by my spirit, says the Lord Almighty."*

To kill a spiritual giant in your life you cannot fight with physical strength, you have to fight with spiritual strength, the power of the Holy Spirit. Many described David in different ways — Jesse his father, his brothers, King Saul, and even the Philistine giant, Goliath, ridiculed and put him down based on his physical appearance.

God said in *1 Samuel 16:7, "Do not consider his appearance or his height".*

The Lord does not look at the things man looks at. Man looks at the outward appearance, but the Lord looks at the heart." No one saw David as a giant killer, but God.

When God called me to the ministry I could have said that I was neither a pastor nor a pastor's son. I didn't even have any training in preaching.

Because of simple obedience to God's gentle call and my willingness to allow him to break and mold my life, he prepared and used me in his vineyard to reach out to many sick, poor, and destitute people. He let me help them come against these giants, physically and spiritually.

I was longing for and crying for God to use me to reach these unreached souls and bring the Gospel of Jesus Christ to their lives. With much prayer and fasting I asked God to direct me to start a ministry. In March 1998, Mathai Outreach Ministry was incorporated in the state of Texas as a charitable Christian organization. The Ministry is based on *Ephesians 1:19, "What is the immeasurable, and unlimited, and surpassing greatness of His power in and for us who believe."* (Amplified Bible) when I read this verse, it opened my eyes and I surrendered to God's promise to do things which I had not done nor experienced so far. By faith, I believed God to open new doors for me to do things for Him. I fully handed over all of my abilities and inabilities to God and obeyed him so that he would direct my path.

The mission of the ministry is based on *Luke 4:18, "[T]o preach the gospel to the poor; he hath sent me to heal the brokenhearted, to preach deliverance to the captives, and recovering of sight to the blind, to set at liberty them that are bruised," (KJV)*

When I looked back at my life, this verse was very true. I was poor and I had lived on the streets as a homeless person. I was sick and brokenhearted. I was in bondage to bad habits and in spiritual darkness. I was physically blind in my right eye. With all of these things, I was hurt in so many ways. When Jesus Christ saved me, he set me free from all of these things. I had a reason to stand against these adversities, or giants, and proclaim the liberty of Christ Jesus to others who are in the same situation I had been in.

In April 1998, on my next mission trip to India, I focused on my people in Pandalam, my hometown. I had called for a Pastor's Conference there and many area pastors, evangelists, and believers came to the hotel auditorium. Pastor K.C. John, the principal of the Mulakuza Bible School, later the overseer of Church of God in India, inaugurated the meeting. We had a wonderful time of praise and worship along with the exposition of the Word of God.

In this meeting I introduced Mathai Outreach Ministry as a grassroots nontraditional, nondenominational, and nonsectarian ministry, but more importantly, as a ministry that was founded on biblical practices. The Word of God and the manifestation of the Holy Spirit as the power of God was demonstrated caused many people to receive salvation. There were also many healed and delivered from demonic possession. I emphasized that this ministry was neither based on traditional practices nor religious doctrines, which often keep sinners away from our Savior Jesus Christ and His Church, but on the word of God.

At that time, we had no limits as to where we could go, and we were willing to go anywhere and ready to work with anyone. Our only desire was to proclaim the Gospel of Jesus Christ and see the deliverance of the people. In that meeting I appointed Pastor Peter P. John as the director of the work in Kerala.

That evening back in my hotel room, while speaking with some guests, I fell asleep. I suddenly experienced a big block of darkness covering the entire area of my room. The intensity of the darkness was such that I could not even see myself. I had never experienced anything like that before. As the darkness descended I saw an image of Sabrimala Sastav, one of the famous deities or gods, who rides the Tiger. They seemed so angry, and the tiger was trying to pounce upon me and claw me. The golden image of this guide is kept in the Pandalam Palace Rajakottaram temple which is a few blocks from where I stayed. This image is carried once a year to Sabrimala where millions go on pilgrimage. As a young person I had been to this temple and stood in front of this image more than once, so I clearly recognized it.

I could not move or do anything as it came down slowly towards me. Though it came close, it had not yet touched me. I struggled in my spirit and body to get rid of this utter darkness. It was so horrible. As the darkness came closer to me I managed to jump out of my bed and began to pray in the Holy Spirit. I began to speak in tongues, battling and rebuking the powers of darkness in the spirit realm.

While I was praying, those who were with me also joined me in prayer. It was spiritual warfare and it went on for almost 25 minutes. The power of darkness was finally defeated by the power of the Almighty God. At last, I felt peace in my spirit and the darkness vanished. Some of the others who were in my room did not understand what had happened.

That dark spirit was a local principality and stronghold of that region. Because of that evil power most of the efforts of evangelism had not been able to prosper. Although many came to do gospel work, none really prospered or continued with the enthusiasm with which they had started.

This demonic spirit was rebuked and defeated by the power of the Holy Spirit. After the spiritual battle, most of my physical strength was exhausted, but we continued in prayer throughout the night. Pastor Peter joined with me that night and the Spirit of the Lord began revealing many things to us through prophecy. The Spirit of God was assuring me of the purpose for which I had been sent to that region, to do the Lord's work. I was to reach the thousands of people who had not heard the Gospel or experienced the deliverance from spiritual bondage.

In spite of everything, God was choosing me to take the responsibility for the spiritual growth of my hometown. The Spirit of God revealed the spiritual inheritance he bestowed upon me in the Pandalam area was as that given to an heir. I am a native of Pandalam, born to a prospered, well-known man according to Kerala standards. I could have had my sizable inheritance of wealth from my father, but I had rejected that and had gone away without anything. I had never wanted any of the inheritance. I have always thought that God has blessed me with everything I needed; I did not want to add anything to that from anyone except God so that I could glorify God for what and who I was in Him.

Then I remembered *1 Kings 3:12, "I will do what you have asked. I will give you a wise and discerning heart, so that there will have never been anyone like you, nor will there ever be."*

He promised that the gospel work was going to prosper and that He was going to bring many faithful people to work and win souls there.

As a confirmation to start a church, God promised there would be 100 new souls from all walks of life coming to receive healing, salvation, baptism and to support a local church within the year. There was limited, if any, new growth in the Pandalam area. I felt it was impossible in the human sense, but we stayed in faith since it was the promise of God.

The very next day, early in the morning, while we were still praying, a young man walked into my hotel room. I did not know him but the other pastor recognized him. I asked him to sit down on the floor with us. I tried to tell him that we were praying for the souls in the area. He sat with us and listened. By the time we finished praying this young man was sobbing.

We shared the Gospel and God's plan for his life with him. He gladly received Jesus into his heart and as soon as he heard about water baptism he wanted to be baptized. Later I found out that he was one of the leading members of the Hindu fanatics and anti-Christian groups in the area. The very next day he invited us to his house and some of his neighbors came with severe asthma, thyroid tumors, juvenile diabetes and many other sicknesses. God healed these people almost instantly and they were very eager to know more about the power of this God who was able to heal them from their sicknesses.

They had served many different gods in the past but those gods only gave them sickness, poverty and bondage. When they heard about Jesus Christ and the power of God they accepted him, his healing and deliverance. These life-changing experiences encouraged other people to come forward and invite us to visit their homes and pray for the sick there too. Very soon, many people came and began to experience the life-changing power of Jesus Christ.

With Pastor Peter and a few other new believers, we started to go to houses, hospitals, and wherever the sick and oppressed were. God's mighty hand worked among the people. Until then I had not baptized any people in Pandalam or Kerala. The Spirit of the Lord encouraged me through this work to start baptizing people. My first convert came forward and was baptized. We had three other baptisms that same week. Even though I did not know many Kerala customs among the Pentecostals nor their traditional way of ministry, the Word of God and the Holy Spirit encouraged, guided, and strengthened me to do many things which I had not done before. Pastor Peter, an ordained minister, was with me and assisted me in many things.

We conducted our very first worship service the next Sunday morning at Pandalam's Marthoma Center. Among the congregation, there were newly saved, baptized, and healed believers who had never attended any other church before. That is how the work got started in Pandalam. Our new believers and Pastor continue to work and experience the same power of God that moved among the people. Within a few days, there were many deliverances and baptisms, and people began to come and worship with us. Many people in the Pentecostal churches began questioning what we were doing. They didn't agree with us doing things outside of their traditions. We focused on what God called us to do and continued to work. We had not invited any other churches or their members to join us.

At that time we did not have a place in Pandalam to stay, so we stayed at the Shines Hotel while we were there. When we returned to the hotel after visiting people, there were usually only a few roadside coffee shops open. Sometimes, there was no food ready even when we found one open, so we had nothing to eat except thattu dosa (bread from rice flour sold by street vendors) and coffee for our meals.

When it was time for me to return to the United States, God's assurance was with me the entire time. On my way back while I was waiting in the Bombay airport, I met a young man from Helsinki, Finland and shared the Gospel with him. He accepted Jesus and went back to Finland. The next day I reached Paris. Dr. Heinz had already arranged my train ticket from Paris to Baden, Switzerland where I'd meet up with some friends. When I arrived in Paris, France I had two large suitcases, a briefcase, and a camera bag. My plan was to leave them in a locker at the airport and continue to travel. I looked many places but there were no lockers available so I had to carry all of my luggage.

One person I was going to see was my friend Ruth. It had been 34 years since we had last seen each other. Ruth and I had worked together in Mangalore in 1964 to 1966. She was only 19 years old when she first came to India and I had not seen her since then, even though I had visited Switzerland before.

We met at the train station in Bern and spent several hours talking about the past. She knew me when I had only one set of clothes. And, at that time, we were very good friends. Ruth had taught me how to dive into the ocean. I remembered her sincere love for human beings. She seemed to be really fascinated with my testimony and the way the Lord directed my paths. She was not happy with her life. She had a failed marriage and was facing other problems in her life. She was also a heavy smoker. My story encouraged her, but when I asked her to surrender her life to Christ the same way I had, she told me I was trying to convince her with little. Then I quoted the Bible words spoken by King Agrippa who was speaking to Paul in *Acts 26:28,29 Then Agrippa said to Paul, "Do you think that in such a short time you can persuade me to be a Christian? Paul replies, "Short time or long – I pray God that not only you but all who are listening to me today may become what I am, except for these chains".* She listened to everything very carefully.

After dinner, we said goodbye and departed that evening. I am sure that she thought about a comforting Savior and accepted him into her life. I found out later through a friend, Conrad, that a few months after I met with Ruth, she was diagnosed with cancer of the throat. She died within four months. It was not easy for me to hear about her death. I realized the love of God for Ruth because he had given me an opportunity to reach out to her with the Gospel of Jesus Christ after 34 years apart. Despite all the difficulty I had traveling from one country to another, it was worth it all just to be able to bring the saving grace of Jesus Christ to one more person. I stand in awe by the ways of God.

That same night after visiting Ruth, I went to see Dr. and Mrs. Heinz. They welcomed me in their home and cared for me. The next evening I left Switzerland to return to Houston by way of Paris.

While I was away, Pastor John Osteen had called my home to inquire about my whereabouts. I met with him when I came back and shared what I was doing and the way God had blessed my ministry. He was very happy with what I was doing. Soon after that visit, Pastor Osteen ordained me as a minister of the Gospel of Jesus Christ and as a member of the clergy at Lakewood Church.

Chapter 11

Church planting

The work at Pandalam started to progress rapidly. I began to feel the responsibilities of being a minister. It was a big transition from being a believer to be a minister, especially with all the work involved in founding the organization. I began to pray that God would give me enough wise and understanding people to lead His work. For the next few months, we did not have a base in Pandalam other than the Marthoma Center, which we were renting. Eventually Pastor Peter found an apartment in the area to live. Many more workers started to join the outreach team. Many of our believers who were healed and delivered joined the team and started to witness to their neighbors and friends. Many people got saved, healed, baptized, and joined the church.

On December 18, 1998, I left again for India. This time, I traveled through South Korea and visited Pastor David Yonggi Cho's church, Yoido Full Gospel Church in Seoul. It is the largest church in the world. I attended one of their worship meetings and the prayer meeting in the prayer mountain where thousands and thousands of people cry out to God for the salvation of people, as well as for church growth. I had the opportunity to sit down and pray with them for the lost souls all around the world. My next stop was Singapore, where I saw hundreds of people of Indian origin wandering on the streets, doing menial jobs or Cooley work. The Spirit of the Lord gave me a burden to reach out to these people.

I arrived in Pandalam two days before Christmas in 1998. On December 22, I marked 30 years since I had gotten saved in 1968. After 30 years, I was back at the same place I had begun my Christian walk, my hometown of Pandalam. I planned to spend my Christmas and New Year's Day in the mission field, but it would be my first time away from my family during the holiday season. A few days before Christmas, I watched the Christmas celebrations in different countries.

In America, Christmas celebrations begin right after Thanksgiving Day. Most people get so busy with shopping, decorating, and wrapping presents that, in my opinion, many people have forgotten or do not even know what Christmas really means. When I went to Pandalam, no one was shopping for Christmas. There was no fanfare and no celebrations. I decided to get together with my team and celebrate the true meaning of Christmas.

We went to every village in the Pandalam area. We rented a van with a PA system and loudspeaker. A group of us took a music team with all the instruments and conducted open-air meetings in every village. There we proclaimed the true meaning of Christmas and preached the gospel. Between December 24 and 25th we covered most of the area. Day and night, we held many public meetings and several cottage meetings. The Spirit of the Lord worked in our midst. People all over the area experienced salvation, healing, deliverance, and baptism. During that trip we had 36 baptisms and many of them joined the church.

One person who was baptized in water was my first cousin, Achankunju from Wyandu. For many years, I had gone there to witness to them. He had accepted Jesus as his personal Savior in one of my previous meetings, but he had put off water baptism all these years. He had been a businessman for almost 40 years and he was very respected in his community. He and his family loved me very much. They would do anything for me. But when it came to baptism, they told me that they believed that they had already been baptized once by sprinkling and did not need to be baptized again.

However, this time, he came voluntarily and traveled a day and a half to be where I was. When he asked me to baptize him, I could see a big change in his life. He was really obeying the Word of God and he had surrendered his life to God. Baptizing him was one of the most joyous moments in my life. It reminded me of John the Baptist baptizing Jesus in the River Jordan. My cousin was the first one to be baptized in water from Wyandu among his family. His wife and two children were very strong denominational Christians and they had told me before that they would never be baptized. I continued to pray for them but I did not expect anything to happen.

Many new pastors and evangelists joined our outreach team at Pandalam under the leadership of Pastor Peter. While I was there, I had called for a worker's meeting and appointed a team of about 15 people to different parts of the Pandalam area. Many people came forward from different religious backgrounds including Hindus, Muslims, and denominational Christians. Many received the word of God and obeyed him by being baptized in water. Many of them also joined the church. As the church grew, our needs grew as well. With the little we had, our team worked day and night with the goal to deliver people from the grip of the enemy. Many miracles and wonders took place, and continue to do so, around the area. On my return to the States, I stopped off in Taiwan where I had a Chinese friend with whom I had studied hospice care in England. He was a highly respected medical doctor. We met and I shared the Gospel with him and we prayed together.

Loss of a great man

I arrived back in Houston on January 8. The next day at church I found out that Pastor John Osteen was very ill and had been in and out of the hospital. I remember Pastor Osteen coming to the stage that day to present the speaker, Pastor T.L. Osborn, with a check. Unfortunately, that would be the last time I would see Pastor Osteen. A few days later he had a massive heart attack and was admitted into the hospital. On January 23, a Saturday afternoon, Renée, Pastor Osteen's secretary, called my house to inform me of Pastor's condition and asked me to pray. Immediately I got ready to go to church and pray with the others. Just then the mailman brought an envelope in the mail that contained a three-year ministerial ordination card signed by Pastor John Osteen.

While I was driving in the car, I pleaded with God to spare his life. All of the sudden I asked loudly, "Why Lord?" I do not know why I questioned God in such a manner, but my heart ached for the potential loss of a man I genuinely admired. I arrived at the church and prayed for several hours, until the news of his death arrived. His death alone was a devastating thing to my whole family. Not just because he was our Pastor, but he was a man who genuinely loved people, especially the people of India. Pastor John Osteen often talked about wanting to live longer to preach the Gospel. He loved India and always wanted to go back to preach the gospel.

We lost a great man of God who had fulfilled his purpose and reached the goals he set out in his life. On the way back home I was still crying in my car. Then I thought about how

I had questioned the Lord. In my own life, so many things had happened to me, but I never questioned God.

When I had first attended the pastors and leaders conference in 1996, it was a time for questions and answers. I took the piece of paper and wrote the question, "Who will be the Pastor of this church when Pastor Osteen is not here?" The question came from a human thinking. I remembered where God had promised King David that if he walked upright, God would raise up heirs to sit on the throne. After hearing the faith building and encouraging words of the Pastor, I did not pass the card up to be answered. The Sunday after Pastor John's death, I saw Joel and Dodie Osteen and their courage and strength to withstand such a moment. I really understood that it had to be God who gave them the strength and courage. Even though I was very sad, and I wholeheartedly wept at his funeral service, I knew in my heart that God was going to keep this church, and the Osteens, very strong. We decided in our heart to stand with this church and the Osteen family.

In June 1999, I returned to the mission field. The Spirit of the Lord told me to go through Dubai in the Persian Gulf. I did not know anyone to visit in Dubai, nor did I have any other purpose in going there. In Dubai, the Christians go to church on Friday. I went to the hotel and I asked the Lord to direct me. The temperature outside was 118°F. I thought that there would be no way I could go out and enjoy my stay. After I arrived, I made some phone calls to local pastors, but I could not get in touch with anyone., so I went to sleep.

At about three in the afternoon the Spirit of the Lord woke me up to pray. While I was praying, one of the pastors I had called in the morning called back and invited me to attend his fellowship meeting in the evening. Dubai is a large cosmopolitan Islamic city with a multinational and multiracial population. There was a large concentration of Indian, Pakistani, Sri Lankan, Bangladeshi, and Filipino workers. There were also many Indian church groups. They all gathered in the same compound with different buildings. Each building had several rooms. Each group assembled for two hours and then the next group would come in.

While attending the meeting, I discovered that there were 200,000 Cooley workers (day laborers) who lived off of low-paying jobs. They lived in a colony in a slum-like neighborhood in very unsanitary sheds or huts. The Spirit of the Lord gave me a burden concerning these people who needed to be reached. I made some inquiries and I got the chance to invite several of them to my hotel room and share the gospel with them. They accepted Jesus as their personal savior. Then I understood why the Lord had led me to go through Dubai.

I continued my journey to India where we were very busy. There were many people who wanted to meet with me and hear the word of God individually, in families, or groups. There were baptisms and several meetings within the small and large groups. The Lord was working in our midst and many people got saved, healed, and baptized.

We had several different kinds of ministries that God was working through, especially the casting out of demons. It was a fairly new experience for me. I had seen the deliverance of people from demon possession, but it was my first time to physically hear demons cry out as they left a person's body when they were commanded to leave in the name of the Lord Jesus Christ. Even though many may not know the powerful name of Jesus, it was amazing to see the evil spirits confessed who they were and then leave with great fear at the very name of Jesus. Through this ministry, many people were delivered and baptized into the church.

Reaching my people

After being baptized in water, my cousin Achankunju immediately went back to his hometown and joined a local Bible school for theological studies, without my knowing.

He was so eager to know more about his newly found faith. Even though he was a wealthy and respected businessman, a deacon at his church, a leader in the community, and had a large family circle, when he came to know the truth and the joy of salvation everything changed for him. He was like Zacchias who left everything and ran to Jesus. This time his wife, Joyce, his daughter Alice, and one of my other nieces, Linnet came from Nilambur to Pandalam along with him to be baptized in water. After their baptism, they invited me to Wynadu.

We traveled a day and a half to get to Wynadu. It was one of my more difficult trips because on the way we got food poisoning and became very ill. Someone also pick pocketed my wallet in the bus station. I had reason to be discouraged and leave, but God strengthened me. We went around and conducted several meetings and house visits. Three of my other cousins and their families came forward and accepted Jesus into their lives and we baptized them there. Many of my other family members attended the meeting and we were able to conduct their first worship service in Sulthan Battery and a similar team started to reach our people there.

I would like to say a few things about the condition of my people at Wynadu. I had a special interest in that place because most of my cousins and their families migrated to Wynadu in the early 1960s. In the late 1990's there were more than 50 families there. They went for economic reasons and most of them were very successful. They were early settlers and had acquired a lot of land and businesses that helped them make money. In the beginning, many denominational churches came and influenced their lives and they became very religious, but lost. Whenever I went to India I had a genuine desire to reach out and bring the saving grace of Jesus to them. That is why I considered that place my personal mission field for a very long time. My people loved me and respected me even though they were very strong reli-

139

gious people. Other people could not go and change them because they would not listen to anyone else. I considered it my personal responsibility to do so.

However, when I began a worship service there, I started to get pockets of resistance from some of my own people because of the influence of their church and affiliation. During one of my mission trips in 1997, I went to visit Wynadu in Northern Kerala where the gospel has not reached compared to South Kerala. The Spirit of the Lord directed me to go to Sulthan Battery where I had many cousins.

The Lord told me to fast three days while staying there, and I obeyed. On the way I saw a vision of a horrible looking dead creature, but I did not understand what the meaning of the vision was. As soon as I arrived there I met one of my first cousins, whom I had not seen since 1967, over 30 years ago. He was said to be the wealthiest man among all of us.

When I saw him, he had lost everything due to drinking, drugs, gambling and other bad habits. He had lost all his strength and he lived in a mud hut with his family. When I looked at him I remembered the dead creature from my vision. I decided to go to his house and I told him that we were going to have a Gospel meeting in his house. This was something he never would have liked or allowed before.

Since I was his first cousin and we had not seen each other for many years, he agreed. In that meeting after hearing the word of God in **Mark 16:16 *"Whoever believes and is baptized will be saved, but whoever does not believe will be condemned."*** I invited all of our relatives to come with me, many would be going to his house for the first time. In short, this man got saved, he repented of his sins and agreed to live a Godly life. The next day I took him to a local Pentecostal church. He testified there and agreed to be water baptized after the service. I invited a pastor to his house to talk with him about baptism. My three days were over and I left that same afternoon.

Later I was told that he had gone to the church to be baptized but the pastor did not think he was prepared enough in the doctrinal knowledge regarding baptism and did not allow him to get baptized. Their church policy was they wouldn't baptize people who didn't have knowledge of their church doctrine. After several weeks he stopped going to that church and went back to his old ways. He was back slidden.

Throughout the bible we see that immediately after getting saved they walk into the baptism. The Apostle Paul, the Ethiopian Eunich, the jailer and many more in the New Testament church. *Acts 16:33 – "And he took them the same hour of the night, and washed their stripes; and was baptized, he and all his straightway." (KJV)*

The lack of vision for the lost souls, lack of soul winning and the lack of desire for soul winning has stunted the growth of the churches there. Most of these churches are looking for perfect people to be their members. We cannot limit the Lord with this kind of attitude. The Lord came with an unconditional love to save the world *John 3:16 "God so loved the world that he gave his one and only Son, that whoever believes in him shall not perish but have eternal life."*

Where is the place for a lost sinner in your church?

On my next trip to that place, I met this man infected with tuberculosis, unable to do anything including getting into the water to be baptized. This missed opportunity saddened me very much. I lost one more of my people from entering into the Kingdom of God. Like him, there are millions of souls who are lost for eternity because of the church doctrines, which keep sinners out of the church. For many, it is a job to preach the Gospel, and they do everything according to the instructions they have been given.

The people who preached strict holiness, and other non-biblical doctrines as the basis for membership of their church, need to understand that it is not their doctrine, or

141

other denominational spirit, that saves the sinner, but it is the blood of Jesus which washes away the sins of the people. It is the love of Christ that brings the sinner to saving grace. It was my hope that they would realize this fact, sooner or later.

During that trip we baptized 44 people. I left India to come back home after a few weeks there, but I had to stop over in Holland. I traveled from Holland to Belgium by bus. I sat at the front of the bus on the left side. It was really nice and sunny throughout the day. As the day progressed, the sun shone on me.

Once we stopped I moved to a seat on the right side of the bus. All of a sudden the clouds began to move in and it became very dark and rainy. The tour guide on the bus noticed this and said to me "Sir you were sitting in that seat and when you sat there it was bright and sunny. But when you moved it became dark and rainy. Would you mind going back and sitting in your old seat?"

"If it will help." I replied.

I moved my seat and we began to talk. She explained to me that she feels the darkness when she goes to her home. So I told her about Jesus, the Light of the world. On our bus ride home, I had the opportunity to share the Gospel with Karin and she accepted Jesus as an American lady also joined with us. We prayed for Karin, that the darkness that oppressed her would go. It went out and she felt very happy.

I was so happy that the Lord used me there. It seems like such an impossible opportunity, but the Spirit of the Lord worked and it was very easy. The very next day I left the Netherlands. I was amazed at the way the Lord was using me. My desire to serve him increased daily. Many days I cried out to God to use me more for his glory. Since I returned from that trip I felt an even stronger sense of responsibility and burden to reach more people in other countries.

Chapter 12

Harvest 2000

W hen I came back from my trip to India in July of 1999 many changes began taking place in my business. New government regulations of the home healthcare industry brought new problems, one after another. The home health-care division of the company was a firmly established, but after 12 years, we had to close it down. Our bills continued to pile in, the government payments did not. Medicare was preventing us from collecting on many of our accounts, and vendors were asking me to pay bills that I'd personally guaranteed.

When I was in India, God revealed many things through prophetic messages through a servant of God I'd met for the first time. God's hand began working more in my life so that I could start serving him more and more. I had recorded the prophetic message, and when I faced trials and problems, I would play it back and listen to the strengthening words of God. These words sustained me when the problems came. I did not depend on it, but rather I trusted God to protect me and everything else I had. I was able to handle each problem in a way that kept me from being stressed. I was also able to push back thoughts of giving up. Slowly God opened new financial opportunities to pay off all the debt.

The only active business we had was the hospice care company. Even in that business there were audits, legal and enforcement actions and other scrutiny. Humanly thinking, I had no opportunity to think of leaving my work to go anywhere else. I prayed and trusted God to open doors. On October 29, 1999 at 3:30 a.m., the Spirit of the Lord woke me up to begin praying and revealed things to me about the next mission trip. He gave me a scripture from *Daniel 12:1-3, "Everyone whose name is found in the book will be delivered."*

I took this as a responsibility to add one more person's name to the book of life. On that day I committed whatever time I have left on the earth to serve God and to bring the Gospel to the unreached before the Lords return.

That morning I started to make plans for my next mission trip. Since I had not been home for the previous year's holiday season, I planned my trip for after Christmas and the New Year.

Y2K

As we were entering into a new and exciting time in human history, a new millennium, new century and a new year, the world was watching and waiting with a lot of uncertainty and despair. As you may remember, people everywhere were afraid of what was going to happen when January 1, 2000 began. A few years earlier, technology had discovered that there was a problem with the computers that managed almost all aspects of human life, especially in developed countries. Many scholars predicted catastrophe with Y2K. The media became very concerned with the effects of Y2K. As it was nearing, all the world governments, scientists, technologists, and businesses got more and more concerned about entering the new millennium. Most people did something to prepare themselves to survive any kind of disruption in their routines, by getting extra supplies of food, water, and other necessities.

As a child of God and a Bible believing Christian, it was an opportunity to trust in the Word of God and His mighty power. No matter what happened in the world, the great assurance we had in Christ Jesus encouraged me to separate more time for God's work. I made plans to go to the mission field in the beginning of the New Year for two months. I had never been gone that long before. The amount of responsibility I had never allowed much time for me to be away from work at home. I had to make many preparations for my trip.

In the past, leaving for a span of three to four weeks was manageable with my staff present to take care of the hospice program. But this time I was going to be gone for two months without a way to reach me. Therefore I had to hire new people and train them to take my place, especially since it was a 24 hour responsibility.

In 1999, we had several audits and problems with the government regulations. On top of this, we were dealing with legal enforcement. This turned out to be very time consuming and paperwork had to be updated on a daily basis. I had to hire new staff and consultants who were qualified to work in several areas. Then I had to train all the new hires. These jobs were highly specialized and it was very hard to find the appropriate personnel. Finally, several months before my trip, I got everyone in place.

The day before I was to leave on my trip, my head nurse manager, who was supposed to take charge in my absence, came to my office at about 11 a.m. and said that she could not, and would not, accept the responsibility. I tried to talk to her and reassure her that she could do the task, but she refused. This was less than 18 hours before my departure. She was a key person and I had no one else to take her place.

I really did not know what to do because I had never antici-
pated that such a thing could happen at that time. I went to
my office, closed the door and sat for a few minutes.

The devil brought a lot of thoughts to my mind, like
canceling the trip because it was a voluntary mission trip.
He tried to make me think that I could make a few calls
to the people who were waiting for me in different parts of
the world. Of course they'd understand the situation. I even
thought that maybe nothing would happen if I missed the trip,
and I could try to use the plane tickets for later time. Then
the thought came in my mind that work was more important
because, after all, this was a business that was bringing me
my paycheck. I couldn't leave it to go.

I really did not know what to do. Finally, I put aside all
the thoughts that the devil brought in and I said to God, "You
are the one who opened the door for the trip. Now the devil
is trying to shut it. I need your help." It was about 3 p.m., and
suddenly I thought of calling one of my ex-employees who
had been trained for this work. She had been gone for two
years and I had no address or phone number for her. After
thinking for a little while, I thought of someone who knew
her and I managed to get in touch with her at 6 p.m. I met
with her at her house and explained the situation. She gladly
encouraged me to continue with my plans and assured me
that she would take care of everything. By the time I arrived
home that night it was 8 p.m. Finally, I started packing
for my two-month trip. By the grace of God I left the next
morning at 6 a.m. on January 20, 2000. How wonderful our
God works!

Prior to leaving, the Spirit of the Lord assured me that
it was going to be a blessed trip, that hundreds would be
delivered, and that I was going to baptize over 100 people
on that trip. The places I was traveling to were not Christian
countries, nor favorable to gospel work. Many of these
places were anti-Christian and there was persecution going

on. Every day we read in the newspapers about the persecution of Christians in the anti-missionary activities that took place. Most of the places I was going to had neither traditional church organizations, nor strong support groups. They were also very new to me. But, because God's Spirit had promised it, I believed and trusted in God.

I cast all my cares upon him, because I knew he cared for me. *1 Peter 5:7 " Cast all your anxiety on him because he cares for you."*

I didn't know what to anticipate, but I started my journey. I stopped in Tokyo for one night and the next day I reached Singapore. Brother Sam was waiting for me and took me to their apartment. We had a good time of fellowship and encouragement. That morning a Tamil speaking, young man came to us for prayer. The Lord touched him and delivered him out of a lot of pain and suffering. I had the opportunity to speak at a large church that evening. The pastor graciously introduced me to his congregation where I spoke for the first time in English for an outside church. But despite my inexperience, God helped me to deliver a good message. I spent a couple of more days there and I met with, and ministered to, some really needy people.

After spending a few days in Singapore, I came to Trivandrum, where Pastor Peter was waiting for me. As soon as he saw me, he told me that the Spirit of the Lord had spoken to him saying that on this trip 100 people would be baptized. I simply smiled and then told them that the Spirit of the Lord told me the same thing before I left Houston. Most of the things about our ministry happened in this manner. God would speak to both of us, so that when we get together to work, we remained in one accord.

Starting a new church

That night we stayed in Trivandrum before going to Pandalam where our workplace was. After everyone left my room, I called the front desk to send me some fresh towels. In a few minutes a middle-aged man brought the towels. When he saw my Bible on the bed he asked me whether I was a praying person. I told him I was and offered to pray for him. Then he told me that he had been suffering from severe asthma and he needed deliverance. Before I could pray for him he said he would be right back. I knew by his name that he was a devout Hindu. A few minutes later he came back with one of his coworkers who was a denominational Christian. As soon as he came back into my room he felt much better and started to breathe normally, even before I prayed.

I asked them to sit down and I shared the Gospel with them. The Hindu man accepted Jesus into his life around 2:00 a.m. The other man said he did not need any of this and that he was already a Christian. But, at 6:30 a.m., this man came back to my room and said he had had no peace from the time he had left my room that night. He said he wanted this Jesus Christ to come into his heart. He accepted Jesus and then invited us to his house.

That evening we all went to his house where he had gathered his relatives who were Hindus. All of them accepted Jesus into their hearts and decided to be water baptized. The Lord delivered them from their many sicknesses. The next morning we took the new believers to the Neyyar dam and six people were baptized in water. We left them to go to Pandalam but promised that we would return. A few days later we went again and ministered among the non-Christians, and many more people were saved. We baptized six more people in two days, and thus a new church was started. We pledged to come back and work among them. Like in the early church, God started this work in Trivandrum without our planning it. Whoever heard the Gospel received it gladly and God healed their infirmities.

From the beginning we experienced the power of God in all things we were involved with. We arrived at Pandalam on January 29 and on the 30th we had a pleasant Sunday worship. My cousin, Pastor C.M. Samkutty and his wife from Chicago, joined us that day. That same afternoon another 13 people were baptized in water. The word of God was received very well where ever it was preached. Almost every day we conducted one or more water baptisms. Without any reservations, we went to talk to people in their towns, villages, homes, huts and on the roadside. We prayed for the sick and preach the Good News with boldness. Whoever accepted the Gospel was also baptized and delivered. All of these new souls joined the church.

To baptize people we had no other choice at times but to go into ponds, lakes, rivers, tanks or wherever we could find water to conduct the baptism. People of all levels came forward and we accepted all of them. We saw many mental patients receive instantaneous healing and the crippled began walking. All kinds of sicknesses and diseases were healed in the name of Jesus. Even though there were pockets of resistance, none came forward to do any harm to our people or to us.

After a few days in Pandalam we left for Sulthan Bathery where we had already started to church on my last visit. This time we were with Pastor Raju when we went to Wynadu. He visited our churches to minister very often in Pandalam where he cast demons out of people. This ministry was very essential, especially for the Hindu converts.

The devil claims a lot of authority in their lives because they worshiped these spirits before they came to the saving grace of Jesus Christ. When we arrived in Wynadu we started our work that same evening. In that evening meeting many people were healed and delivered. Among them was a very prominent Hindu family. The father was a businessman and a high-level, local politician. After watching the deliverances in the service, he and his family surrendered their lives to Jesus Christ and made public confession of their experience. Immediately his household was baptized in water along with him. This was a good testimony for that place. After a few days in Wynadu, almost 36 people had been water baptized from different backgrounds and faiths, including high government officials.

Without wasting a day, we all continued to work amongst the people. We also went to Idikki and Munnar, an eastern high range area. There many people got saved. Because of the difficulty in reaching those places, we did not officially start a church there at the time.

On that trip, after 35 years, I also had a chance to spend some time with Dr. and Mrs. Heinz in India. I had a chance to share the mission of serving and reaching out to those who were most needy, something I had learned from him about 37 years earlier.

The team and I returned to Pandalam and started our mini crusade in the villages. Everywhere we went we conducted meetings and went to homes to evangelize. Altogether we baptized about 54 people in Pandalam. At this point, 5 1/2 weeks into our trip, we had baptized 115 people. Many more would have made the decision to be baptized, but we could not reach them in time. The tremendous harvest of souls gathered by doing outreach encouraged and strengthened us to march forward. I also spent a few days with our workers and their individual churches. That was a time for teaching and learning.

While I was there, I realized how important it was that we had the use of the motor vehicle we purchased on my last trip. Lakewood Church had helped us with that purchase. Using the vehicle had helped us to travel to villages. The vehicle had helped us transport the team and equipment. It had also helped take people to and from baptisms. Ladies used the van to change clothes after the baptisms and we were thereby able to avoid confrontations with anti-Christian groups. On this trip alone, about 6000 km were put on the van in a month's time.

On my return trip to the States, I flew through Singapore to Malaysia. Reverend David, an ordained Lutheran priest who was in charge of several churches in Portklang, near the Kuala Lampur area, hosted us. My first meeting was in a Methodist church, and then in a Lutheran one. In both places the Spirit of the Lord enabled me to preach the Gospel. Many people got delivered and received the Gospel.

Malaysia is predominantly a Muslim country. Almost 55% of the population is Muslim and the rest are of Chinese and Indian origin. Even though they speak the Malay language, many people speak English as well as Tamil. Most people I had contact with were Tamil speaking. While we were speaking the priest told me one thing, "I have been preaching to people with what I learned in seminary, but now I see the Spirit of the Lord touching and delivering people." He and his family surrendered their lives to Jesus Christ that day.

They experienced the same deliverance and healing in their lives and decided to be baptized by immersion in water as a whole family. That afternoon he took us to another village church where he was also the priest of the church. There the Gospel was preached and accepted by the congregation. We also were able to pray for the sick and needy and God faithfully met their needs. The next day I left for Panang. From there I went to Singapore and preached in another evangelical church. On these trips I met many godly people who loved Jesus very much. It was a privilege to go to so many places and receive the hospitality of so many.

Harvest 2000, my first mission trip for the millennium, helped me to make a continued commitment to serve the God who had transformed my life. Everywhere we went and ministered, people responded very well. Our non-traditional, non-denominational approach of reaching out to the people who were in need opened many doors for us to minister. We had very little opposition from other religious people to present the unfailing love of Jesus Christ and his resurrection power.

My two months stay with our team was a big encouragement to me and to the workers. We all worked tirelessly every day. We went to different areas and conducted either open air meetings or cottage meetings. Our believers and workers reached out to neighboring villages and brought people to the meetings. As the word of Jesus said *"The harvest is plenty the laborers are few" Matt 9:37*

Every place we went people were anxious to hear and experience healing and deliverance. We continued to be ready to hear the Word of God as it is written in *John 4:35 " ....Open your eyes and look at the fields! They are ripe for harvest."*

The fields are ripe for harvest. The more we worked and the harder we worked, the more villages there were to visit. There are millions of people yet to reach. Instead of feeling satisfied with our accomplishments we felt the deeper responsibility to reach more.

During these times the Spirit of God assured us that within three years we were going to baptize 1000 new souls in the Pandalam area. God promised that once we had 1000 members, God was going to give us a place for worship.

Each day in the mission field was an exciting day to see God's power manifest and to see people experiencing God's power in the church. Even after my return home, our team of dedicated pastors and workers continued to work and new believers continue to be added to the church every day. It was a joy to see the deliverance of my people.

I continue to go back to India to work with our team 1 or 2 times a year. The field is ripe for harvest. While we have the opportunity let us get out of our comfort zone and lead one more person from darkness to light. God continues to use these imperfect vessels of clay for a purpose beyond our understanding, to lead one more person to eternal life through the simple plan of God, the good news of the Gospel.

Chapter 13

Seeking new challenges

Without a challenge it impossible to accomplish anything big or great in the world; this is also true for one's spiritual life. We have to challenge ourselves to reach a certain level or specific standard. The champions always challenge themselves to reach higher. The Master already gives the challenge or the great commission to a child of God. *Matt. 28:19 "Therefore go and make disciples of all nations, baptizing them in the name of the Father and of the Son and of the Holy Spirit."*

As you accept the challenge, God is willing and able to give you what you need to accomplish it. As a leader in both my professional and ministerial life, I have learned to ask God for the wisdom and understanding to guide his people just as King Solomon did in *1 Kings 3:9." So give your servant a discerning heart to govern your people ...."*

I continually ask God to equip me to do his work wherever he sends. From a young age, and especially because of my background, I never really had anyone to depend on but God, even for the smallest things.

When I first heard the voice of God telling me to go back to my people I didn't know where He would send me. I obeyed God and went to many different places and people groups until I found what God wanted me to do. After I took the first step, the challenges began. My first challenge was to identify the enemy and overcome spiritual adversity by fasting and praying. Because I was willing to go, God equipped me to do that by the power of the Holy Spirit. In being faithful in the little things, God enabled me to go on to bigger things.

As the founder of this ministry, my goal is to prepare myself with the needed knowledge and grace to help people. It takes much more consecration than what I have given in the past. I have found that the more opportunities I receive, the greater the responsibility I have towards God and man. I now must be fully committed to what God has called me to do, because I am accountable to many. I must also acquire further education and training in ministerial and biblical knowledge.

A daily challenge I face is surrendering myself fully to Christ so that I can be used only by Him and for His glory. It takes a lot of prayer to find the right people to carry out the work in different areas, especially ones who are willing to be faithful and committed.

When we started working among the sick, oppressed, needy, and poor, many of them received the Gospel gladly and wanted to live faithfully for God and Jesus Christ. Many of these people also paid a big price. They were immediately separated and isolated from their loved ones. They were then identified as people who accepted a foreign and Western God and were subject to all kinds of isolation and persecution.

As a new grassroots ministry, we have had many challenges set before us. We have to depend on God for each and every need we have. Unless you build the foundation on God, whatever you build can fall at any time.

The challenge to the church leaders

No religious doctrine alone has the power to save a sinner. Many religious doctrines mask the power of God and the manifestations of the Holy Spirit. Such religious doctrines keep sinners away from Jesus Christ and His Church. Jesus commanded to you and me to go, to send, and to prepare the laborers. Unless we get out of our comfort zone we cannot go to the masses of the unreached people and bring them the Gospel. Unless we prepare them whom shall we send? We must ask ourselves daily what we did today to reach one person who does not know Christ? We can not say it's our responsibility.

God has been, and is, always looking for willing and obedient people to take up the challenge that He has laid out.

In spite of all the advanced technologies and modern civilization, the crowds we see are lost without hope. They have no assurance of tomorrow and no reason to live.

Knowledge of the saving grace of our Lord Jesus Christ is neither found, nor experienced, by the lost. There is a vast generation gap in the advanced Christian countries. There is no one to look up to, no one to trust. They are lost. As I traveled to most of these countries both Christian and other countries, I see the great need to reach people with the salvation message.

Let us lay aside all these vain religious doctrines and denominational differences, and follow the Master's footsteps to reach the lost generations with the Gospel of Jesus Christ. Let us have compassion on these crowds all over the world. Two –thirds of the world's population – more than 3.2 billion people – live in the 10/40 window. 95% of these people have never been evangelized and are unreached with the Gospel of Jesus Christ. My own homeland, India, has over one billion people but less than 3% are Christians.

157

That is all denominations of Christianity. All surrounding Asian countries are much less than that. That means in these areas 97% of the people do not know Christ as there Savior. What about the Middle Eastern countries, African countries, Scandinavian Countries, Pacific Islands, the so called Christian countries like Eastern and Western Europe, South and Central America, you can imagine all the other countries in this world. If God created man in His own image, are there souls not important to God?

I was told only 2% of Australian people go to church on a regular basis. In American how many of our neighbors and co-workers experience the power of God. *Matt.9:36 "When he saw the crowds, he had compassion on them, because they were harassed and helpless, like sheep without a shepherd."*

Consider investing God's resources to take His message to the unreached millions around the world. Let us get out of our comfort zone and build an army of leaders to touch the lost millions without the knowledge of a loving savior. Let us remember the Masters voice, *Matt. 9:37"Then he said to his disciples, "The harvest is plentiful but the workers are few."*

Challenge to the unbelievers

Sin separated man from the fellowship with God, our maker. The glory of God and His protection left man. God's enemy, the devil and his demon forces, brought the effects of this sin on mankind in the form of sickness, poverty, bondage, and spiritual blindness. But the loving God, in His infinite wisdom, provides a remedy for this lost condition. Jesus came to this world to pay a ransom for our sins, so that you and I don't have to be separated from God, but live with him in eternity which is for a very long time.

In the Bible God promises a future for the children of God, a future filled with the goodness of God. It is a way for man to reunite with God. He sent his only begotten son to die on the cross for you and for me. *"For God so loved the world that he gave his only begotten son, that whosoever believeth in him should not perish, but have everlasting life." John 3:16 (KJV)*

God has a plan in your life, a plan to prosper you, set you free, take the bondage of sin and sickness, or addiction to any kind of habits and mental confusion, you have been trying to be good person but the more you try, the more you are going back! You have no victory in your life because the enemy doesn't want you to be in victory, he wants you in bondage. With God you have a great future.

You saw in my story I was in the same place where you are today. I know what God did in my life and it is my sincere desire that you come to the knowledge of Christ by inviting Him into your life. The Bible says in *2 Corinth. 5:17 "Therefore, if anyone is in Christ, he is a new creation; the old has gone, the new has come!"*

The moment you ask Jesus to come in to your heart, he will forgive all your sins, and wash you with His blood. The enemy has no more claims on your life. *Roman 8:1 "There is now no condemnation for those who are in Christ Jesus."*

You too can experience the full life that God promised to his children.

Rev.3:20 "Here I am! I stand at the door and knock. If anyone hears my voice and opens the door, I will come in and eat with him, and he with me."

WON'T YOU OPEN YOUR HEART FOR JESUS.

AN INVITATION

Ask Jesus Christ to come into your heart.

Accept Him as your Savior,

Find a Bible believing church

And have fellowship with them.

Let the Almighty God help you and bless you.

Chapter 14

Here I conclude

G od is an amazing potter. When the clay reached the potter's hand it has no idea what happens next. The clay simply doesn't have the power to do anything, so I went through the process of breaking, melting, molding, filling and only after that, will it have any use for the potter. As you read my story you have seen what I had to go through in an ordinary everyday life without any short cuts, I had to go through the trials and tribulations and the experience of the pit of destruction, almost the lowest level any individual can go, but the moment I realized and turned from my way and surrendered my life to God, God started to give me a life beyond anybody's expectation. When I look back at my past it has no influence on my present or future because God started fulfilling his promise in the children of Gods life. *Jer.29:11 "For I know the plans I have for you, declares the LORD, plans to prosper you and not to harm you, plans to give you hope and a future."*
Today I have a purposeful life with assurance and hope for the future and able to share that assurance with others. This was just not mere luck or an American dream come true.

Every event took place in my life and there is a footprint in every step I took. This story is not completed, it continues to be a blessing not only to me but to many others around me. I am looking forward to a better tomorrow than yesterday with Gods help.

Today my wife and I have traveled almost 45 countries, mostly in the unreached areas, with the gospel of Jesus Christ. Our desire is to go to the uttermost parts of the world to testify of this Master whose love is unconditional.

What we do

Mathai Outreach Ministries is an International grass root level non-denominational Christian organization. Evangelization, healing, deliverance, outreach and church planting are among the main areas of concentration for this ministry. As Apostle Paul says in **Romans 15:20 "It has always been my ambition to preach the gospel where Christ was not known, so that I would not be building on someone else's foundation."**

Our ministry is now concentrating mostly in India, we have teams of local missionaries reaching the local communities in different states and the language groups. We have several groups and churches in Kerala, Tamil Nadu, Karnataka in South India. Now we are focusing more on the villages of North India based in Maharastra, Gujarat and Rajastan. Besides our outreach programs in the villages we have several churches and Bible training centers, women's center, and elementary education program. Soon we have plans to expand to the neighboring states, Madya Pradesh, Uthar Pradesh, Punjab. We also have plans to reach out to Napal and Bhuttan. We consider that it is a privilege and honor to labor in the vineyard of our Lord.

We hope and pray that this book has blessed you.

We request you to pray for our ministry so that it can fulfill the purpose the Master has.

God bless you

If you need any further information,

Please feel free to write to us:

Mathai Outreach Ministries, Inc.

P.O. Box 96495

Houston, Texas 77213-6495

United States of America

Visit our website:

http://www.mathaioutreach.org

Email us at:

Info@mathaioutreach.org

What they say about this book:

A *Handful of Clay in the Potter's Hand* is a touching story, narrating the life changing experiences of a rebellious runaway, who was later transformed to a true believer, successful entrepreneur, dedicated humanitarian and devoted evangelist. This autobiography is filled with incidents and events that manifest the delivering power of Jesus Christ. Through his use of simple words and vivid recollection of events, Ipe Mathai has created a personal story that nurtures the reader's mind and spirit. I recommend this book to believers and non-believers alike.

Prof. E.C. Samkutty, Ph.D., Louisiana

"The life history of Ipe Mathai is an impressive story of human determination and faith in God."
C Heinz, M.D., Switzerland

"I read your book and it was awesome. I just wrote to thank you, because that book gave me a new vision in my life."
Oscar Acosta M.D., Honduras

"I have finished reading the whole book in a single sitting one night."

Timothy Tan, Singapore

"This book is an awesome testimony of God's work in His faithful children. He is a living miracle, and his life shows how God delights in using a humble heart for His glory and honor."

Manuel & Claudia, Bogota, Columbia

"I was profoundly moved by the account of your life's experiences."

Conrad Edge, Scotland

"It is so interesting that it was hard to stop reading it at bedtime."

Dr. Lyle & Ruth Alloway, Nebraska

"It has such encouragement to us who have this desire to succeed. I would not put it down until I finished it."

David Memba, Nairobi, Kenya

"We appreciate very much you honoring us with this special gift (book)."

Hugh L. McColl, Jr., Chairman and CEO Bank of America, Charlotte, North Carolina

"Your book has been going from hand to hand and hasn't yet returned to me, but It has blessed many."

Lieut. Colonel Vera Williamson, MBE, Feilding New Zealand

"Your story reminds all of us that no matter what the adversity, God still has a perfect plan for each of our lives. Like when you stretch a rubber band back to send a toy sling-shotting across the field, the trial that seem to stop us, or even push us backwards, God uses to catapult us to our future. Thanks for being so open and honest. Your testimony inspires hope in those who have been there, or are there.

Tiffany Colter, Writer and Writing
Career Coach, Ohio

About
Mathai Outreach Ministries

The testimony of Evangelist Ipe Mathai demonstrates that when we turn even the most challenging trial over to God, He can make a miracle out of it.

The passion of Mathai Outreach Ministries is to share the message of Christ. To reach this goal we have flown, driven and walked hundreds of thousands of miles. It has taken us to remote villages where we've preached by candle light and in to the houses of wealthy community leaders. In each place our goal is the same, share the life-changing message of Christ. We go in to many remote areas that are untouched by other ministries.

It is our hearts desire that you commit your life to Christ and experience his love and forgiveness. There is an abundant life ahead of you when you release control and step in to your call. God is sovereign and has a great plan for your life, the one that will bring you the greatest joy and fulfillment.

This is a call and commitment that has begun with one generation and continued to the next. My family and I not only believe in this ministry, but we work in it and for it. We work our jobs to fund this important work but the need is great.

We encourage you to be a part of this ministry through your prayer and support. Your gift will help continue to actively support all aspects of evangelism. 100% of your gifts go to the native mission fields.. While there you can sign up for your semi-monthly newsletter that will provide current updates from the mission field.

For more information visit us at
www.MathaiOutreach.org
Email: info@mathaioutreach.org

"Yet, O Lord, you are our Father.

We are the clay, you are the Potter;

we are all the works of your hand."

Isaiah 64:8

Printed in the United States
132391LV00002B/2/P